A PRACTICAL GUIDE FOR TEACHING THE MENTALLY RETARDED TO SWIM

COUNCIL FOR NATIONAL COOPERATION IN AQUATICS AND
AMERICAN ALLIANCE FOR HEALTH, PHYSICAL EDUCATION, AND RECREATION

aahper
publications

Copyright © 1969

AMERICAN ALLIANCE FOR HEALTH,
PHYSICAL EDUCATION AND RECREATION

01 Sixteenth Street, N.W., Washington, D.C.   20036

O: r from: American Alliance for Health,
        Physical Education, and Recreation
1201 Si   enth Street, N.W., Washington, D.C.   20036
            Stock No. 245-08078

Council for National Cooperation
in Aquatics

The Council for National Cooperation in Aquatics (CNCA), made
of representatives from 27 national voluntary and governmental
agencies, reaches membership constituencies of millions of
people. The idea for expanding cooperative aquatic efforts at
the national level was originated informally in 1945. Following
two years of discussions and successful preliminary meetings,
the Korean conflict stimulated a planning meeting during the
early summer that brought about the organization of CNCA, as now
known, in the fall of 1951. All ages, both sexes, the physically
fit and the unfit, the mentally alert and the mentally retarded
are served through broad programs of aquatics. During the two
decades of its operation CNCA has engaged in significant pro-
jects--general conferences, intensive workshops, scholarship aid,
and publications--that have been of interest to its members,
contributed to health, fitness, safety, and recreation of count-
less persons, stimulated professional and volunteer leadership,
and emphasized its slogan, "Progress Through Cooperation."

American Alliance for Health,
Physical Education, and Recreation

The American Alliance for Health, Physical Education, and
Recreation (AAHPER) is affiliated with the National Education
Association and has a membership of more than 45,000 health
educators, physical educators, and recreation specialists.
Founded in 1885, this Alliance, formerly the American Association for Health, Physical Education, and Recreation, is
concerned with improving the physical education, health
education, and recreational opportunities for children,
youth, and adults throughout the country. Between July 1,
1965, and June 30, 1968, the AAHPER conducted the Project
on Recreation and Fitness for the Mentally Retarded with a
grant received from The Joseph P. Kennedy Jr. Foundation.
On July 1, 1968, the scope of the Project was officially
expanded to encompass all handicapping conditions. The
AAHPER Board of Governors made the Unit on Programs for the
Handicapped a permanent part of its structure and operation
in November, 1968. The scope and function of activities,
services, and materials provided by AAHPER in health, physical
education, and recreation for the handicapped will continue
to expand to meet the needs and demands of all personnel
interested and involved in these programs.

Committee Members

Arthur Bieri
Supervisor of Elementary Physical Education
Stillwater Public Schools, Stillwater, Oklahoma

*Mrs. Wanda L. Burnette, Program Assistant
Programs for Handicapped, AAHPER

Mart Bushnell, Assistant Director
Health and Safety Services, Boy Scouts of America
New Brunswick, New Jersey

Alexander Houston, Director, Safety Services
American National Red Cross
Boston Metropolitan Chapter, Massachusetts

Mrs. Isobel Lea, Director of Aquatics
Metropolitan Toronto Retarded Children's Education Authority
Toronto, Ontario, Canada

*Mrs. Ruth R. Magher, Chairman
Department of Physical Education, Queens College
Charlotte, North Carolina

Dan Meehan, Assistant Director, Safety Program
American National Red Cross, Mile High Chapter
Denver, Colorado

*William Muhl, Principal
Freeman School
Rockford, Illinois

Michael Rand
National Jewish Welfare Board
New York, New York

*William Rapp, Consultant
Federation of Rocky Mountain States, Inc.
Denver, Colorado

*Mrs. Grace Reynolds, Director
Recreation for the Handicapped
Young Men's Christian Association, Longview, Washington

*Julian U. Stein, Consultant
Programs for the Handicapped, AAHPER

Evan M. Thompson, Safety Programs Representative
American National Red Cross, Mid-Michigan Chapter
Lansing, Michigan

* Editorial Committee

CONTENTS

PREFACE

Swimming generally is considered one of the best physical activities for developing and maintaining high levels of physical fitness and is a wholesome recreational activity in which any individual can participate throughout his life. Swimming is looked upon as an excellent activity to meet various needs of the mentally retarded. In addition to contributions swimming makes to physical fitness, motor development, and physical proficiency, it enables participants to experience success and achievement, to gain confidence, to take pride in their accomplishments and in what they are doing, to become more cooperative--and more competitive, to see a task through from beginning to end, and to have fun. For the hperactive water can be therapeutic and quieting; for the hypoactive, it can be an activator and a stimulus for action. Personnel in the field constantly are seeking new materials, different approaches, and fresh ideas to use in both instructional and recreational swimming programs for the retarded.

Swimming is a major topic and area of concern at many workshops, clinics, and institutes dealing with programs for the mentally retarded. Increasing numbers of requests for information and materials about swimming for the retarded are coming to many different agencies and organizations. However, many individuals who have attended and participated in workshops, evaluated materials, and have been involved directly in swimming programs for the retarded have indicated that this is an area in need of attention and development.

A *Practical Guide for Teaching the Mentally Retarded to Swim* has been developed to help fill voids in instructional and recreational swimming programs for the mentally retarded. This publication has resulted from a joint effort of the American Association for Health, Physical Education, and Recreation's Project on Recreation and Fitness for the Mentally Retarded, a part of the Unit on Programs for the Handicapped, and the Council for National Cooperation in Aquatics. These two organizations recognized inadequacies in aquatic and swimming programs for the retarded and commissioned a committee to investigate needs, to assess what was going on around the country, to determine from personnel in the field their most pressing problems, and to take action.

This committee had wide geographical representation; each member was selected for his knowledge, competence, and experience in swimming programs for the retarded. Individual members of the committee were responsible for canvassing a section of the country to obtain materials, ideas, and suggestions for consideration and inclusion in the publication. This information--data collected from interested and dedicated personnel connected with every type of swimming program for the retarded--and ideas drawn from members of the committee were developed into the original manuscript.

During the summer of 1968 a draft of this manuscript was circulated among various agencies for field testing and among selected individuals for reaction. Personnel selected to review the draft included those with a great deal of experience in swimming programs for the mentally retarded, a few just starting programs, some from camp and recreation programs, others from residential facilities and school situations, some who dealt with the educable, and others who taught the trainable. A representative cross section of personnel involved in swimming programs for the retarded reacted to and evaluated the material. Every comment, suggestion, idea, addition, and deletion was reviewed and appropriate action taken by the Editorial Committee.

This *Guide* is a composite of the thinking and experience of many individuals who have taught the mentally retarded to swim. It incorporates the successful, the practical, and the functional into a flexible and workable resource. In no way is this intended to be Utopia, Shangri La, or the way to teach every mentally retarded youngster to swim. A basic premise is that there is no single approach or sequence which will guarantee success for every instructor with every student. The contents of the *Guide* are a point of departure for each instructor who will have to find the most appropriate methods, techniques, and progressions to reach the individuals and classes for which he is responsible. Information in this *Guide* is intended to help instructors formulate well defined plans of action for their specific situations, and to stimulate imagination, trigger creativeness, and encourage initiative. Instructors content with the *status quo* are destined to stagnation and regression; those granted the privilege of teaching the mentally retarded constantly must look for new avenues and approaches so that they can be more effective in fulfilling their mission.

Although this publication has been developed to help personnel who teach the mentally retarded to swim, and many of the special techniques, devices, and progressions discussed have been devised to meet special and unique needs of the retarded, these same approaches and methods are appropriate for and applicable to non-retarded who encounter the same problems in learning to swim and who function at comparable levels. The emphasis of this publication upon programs for mentally retarded does not imply lack of concern for the physically or multiply handicapped. Needs of the mentally retarded dictated this approach since the mentally retarded comprise about three-quarters of all who have limiting conditions and since special programs developed for the retarded can later be adapted and applied to the multiply handicapped. The immediate need is for new, innovative, and original approaches to help the retarded develop a sound swimming base before being introduced to other aquatic activities. The urgency to refine, enrich, and upgrade swimming programs for the retarded was not expressed as much by personnel working with those having other handicapped conditions.

Every day the progress and achievements of mentally retarded boys and girls and men and women who have been given opportunities to participate in programs designed to meet their specific needs amaze everyone. Achievement in physical and motor activities has stimulated, triggered, and motivated many retarded to heights not thought within their capabilities. Dedicated instructors have offered themselves in a worthy cause, and, in so doing, have accomplished the unthinkable, reached the untouchable, and taught the unteachable--one cannot foresee the waves of influence which may come from a single pebble dropped into water! From humble beginnings wonderous things happen; and who knows, a youngster first reached through his successes in swimming may attain unimagined goals in any one of many areas. It is with these thoughts and with the hope and conviction that the future for the retarded is brighter than anyone can anticipate or predict that this *Guide* is dedicated.

Innovation isn't novelty but annihilation of established structure.

Since this is a working document, it will be subject to future revision--sections will be changed, others will require additions, and still others will need deletions as situations and conditions change. Users of this *Guide* are asked to assist in future revisions by sending their suggestions, reactions, and ideas for addition and deletion to the AAHPER Consultant on Programs for the Handicapped, 1201-16th Street, N.W., Washington, D. C., 20036.

SWIMMING AND THE MENTALLY RETARDED

Students at St. Coletta School, Jefferson, Wisconsin, have fun and learn that water can be their friend.
Mr. Robert McCoy, Milwaukee, Wisconsin

This publication has been designed to help professionals and volunteers teach
the mentally retarded to swim or to swim better. The importance of respect
for, and appreciation and understanding of safe water practices is emphasized
as well as the techniques and approaches for teaching swimming. Material
included will help instructors provide developmental sequences of activities
which are enjoyed by mentally retarded individuals as they are challenged
to improve their swimming skills, their knowledge of aquatics, and their
attitudes in and about water.

The Mentally Retarded

Mental retardation is a condition of mental arrest or lack of mental development which may be present at birth or acquired as a result of disease, accident, or deprivation. Mental retardation is an impairment which is most apparent in academic activities or in traditional classroom pursuits. Mentally retarded individuals have the potential for exhibiting the same range of abilities as the non-retarded in performing physical and motor activities. However, the ability to perform physical and motor activities is generally related to the degree of arrested intellectual function and may result in poor physical and motor performance.

Mental retardation affects one of every thirty people in the United States. Over six million people in this country are retarded. It disables ten times as many as diabetes, twenty times as many as tuberculosis, twenty-five times as many as muscular dystrophy, and six hundred times as many as infantile paralysis before the Salk vaccine! With such a large segment of the population classified as mentally retarded, almost everyone has some contact with a retarded child or adult and many more people are becoming concerned with problems faced by the retarded. During the past decade much progress has been made in helping the mentally retarded adjust to society and in making society more knowledgeable, appreciative, and understanding of his condition. Nationally, regionally, and locally there is a continuing and growing concern for the health, physical fitness, and recreational needs of the mentally retarded. This is exemplified by programs sponsored by the National Association for Retarded Children (NARC), President's Committee on Mental Retardation, President's Council on Physical Fitness and Sports, The Joseph P. Kennedy, Jr. Foundation, American Association for Health, Physical Education, and Recreation (AAHPER), Council for Exceptional Children (CEC), American Association on Mental Deficiency (AAMD), and the many aquatic organizations represented by the Council for National Cooperation in Aquatics (CNCA).

The mentally retarded are generally classified and grouped for educational purposes according to mental ability.

The *educable mentally retarded (EMR) or mildly retarded* usually attend public schools and are frequently educated in special education classes. This category represents the largest group of mentally retarded, with approximately 25 of every 30 retardates classified as mildly retarded. Many EMR's need no special grouping, adaptation, or modification to realize success and progress in instructional swimming programs. Most retarded students who function as retardates because of deprivation will make progress in regular programs without any modification being necessary. Some educables will need specialized instruction in beginning stages until they become semi-skilled; many may then participate safely and successfully in regular swimming classes. Some EMR's due to an added physical or emotional problem will need to have constant special attention, often with student and teacher on a one-to-one basis.

The *trainable mentally retarded (TMR) or moderately retarded* number four of every 30 retardates and constitute the second largest group. Trainable mentally retarded persons are increasingly being cared for in the community, where they may attend special schools and participate in sheltered workshop programs. Most TMR's are semi-dependent and even though they may remain in the community through their adult life, they need a great deal of support, supervision, and assistance. A portion of the moderately retarded group live in residential facilities and require direct supervision throughout their lives. Experience has shown that most trainable mentally retarded persons can learn to swim, can succeed in supervised aquatic programs, can derive enjoyment and can experience physical, social, and emotional benefits from swimming activities.

The *severely retarded, custodial, or profoundly retarded* are generally totally dependent and seldom achieve mental development much above a normal three-year old child. Retardates in this group are seldom found living at home or participating in activities in the community. However, a large percentage of severely retarded can profit from supervised aquatic activity and this activity provides one of the few recreational outlets available to them. The therapeutic values of swimming and aquatic activity are especially beneficial for this group.

Research and experience are showing that swimming and related aquatic skills can be important factors in helping to satisfy the health, fitness, and recreational needs of the retarded. Swimming provides an opportunity for each retardate to enjoy water, achieve success in enjoyable motor skills, and to participate socially in a meaningful group activity.

The number of success experiences for the mentally retarded may be to a large degree limited by the extent of the mental deficit. Since the retardate is generally closer to being "normal" in physical function than in any other area, his greatest success potential probably lies in physical and motor activities. Most retardates, regardless of level, age, or background, are able to experience some degree of success in aquatic activities. An improved self-image, associated with success in swimming, can have a marked influence on the retardate's total behavior pattern. Motivation and interest associated with success in swimming does carry over into other facets--mental as well as physical-- of the retardate's life. Swimming provides a lifetime recreational outlet for the retarded and gives them opportunities for wholesome social experiences which can lead toward their acceptance by others in the community. In spite of their tendency for physical normalcy, many retardates are less physically fit than their non-retarded contemporaries. This generally is a result of the lack of opportunity to participate in physical and recreational activities. Swimming provides an excellent medium for improving muscle tone, organic strength, and motor ability and therefore can be an important factor in the total physical development of the retardate.

3

Evaluation: Basis for Individualization

Every retarded student in swimming classes must be evaluated in terms of his mental, physical, social, and emotional make-up. Although there is much overlap in physical abilities among those in the different classifications, usually the greater the mental deficiency the greater is the likelihood of poor physical fitness, substandard corrdination, and the possibility of secondary impairments such as speech, hearing, and visual problems. There are numerous exceptions, so the instructor can expect to find some students with average and above average physical abilities in all retarded categories.

It is possible for an individual retardate to have sufficient physical ability to permit his participation in normal swimming teaching situations; however, inadequate social and/or emotional development might well cause this placement to bring about failure and frustration. All personal, social, and emotional characteristics of the individual must be assessed to help determine the best approach to be used in teaching him to swim. Other personal factors which can help in determining the approach to be used include the student's attitude toward water, his drive and desire, and the motivation and interest which he exhibits.

The instructor should have knowledge of the student's academic, home, and community life so he can make swimming instruction compatible with and related to his other experiences. Student-instructor rapport is necessary for success and with some retardates takes time to develop. Rapport is difficult to establish when a student changes instructors constantly. Therefore, when a harmonious relationship is established, it should be continued as long as it is beneficial to the student. A case study record provides the instructor with the opportunity to record student progress, to report behavior patterns, and serves as a teaching device designed to build a logical pattern of swimming skills and attitudes. Individual and collective class characteristics are important in helping determine student readiness and placement and must be considered before setting up individual or group teaching sequences.

Teaching the retarded to swim is not markedly different from teaching the non-retarded; sound teaching techniques are important in reaching both groups. In teaching the retarded more concern must be given to breaking down skills and their component parts into small meaningful units; all teaching must be interesting and motivating to the student and the instructor must be perceptive to the signals signifying that learning is no longer taking place. Each lesson should be challenging and fun for every student; motivation can be kept at a high level by having each lesson diversified and interesting.

Every student, regardless of his ability or level, should experience some success in each lesson (*Planned achievement*)--the swimming program must not be another source of failure and frustration for the retarded. *Planned recognition* needs to go along with planned achievement. Recognition of success is important to the retardate and must be a part of the program if instruction is to be successful and meaningful.

Instructors should consciously use a multi-sensory approach in which visual, auditory, tactile, and kinesthetic stimuli are used individually or in combination to reinforce learning and to make use of every avenue of learning. Retarded students learn best by doing; maximum student activity and participation is necessary during every lesson if interest is to be maintained and the instruction is to be successful.

The physical environment must be conducive to learning; any conditions which might detract from the learning process should be eliminated. Some elements of a good learning environment for swimming include a good facility (pool or lake site), appropriate water and air temperatures, suitable water depth, a sufficient number of trained instructors and aides, and adequate supervision and help in locker and shower rooms. A safe, secure, and enjoyable atmosphere is an important component of the teaching-learning process.

The Instructional Staff

Swimming programs which have most successfully reached the retarded generally have an adequate staff consisting of one or more trained instructors who teach skills and direct the program and a number of parents or volunteers who assist with actual instruction. There are many desirable qualities for swimming instructors and considerations for training them. The trained and skilled instructor should--

1. Have a broad base of aquatic knowledge and skill.

2. Complete a recognized swimming instructor training course if possible and have additional training and experience in swimming programs for the handicapped.

3. Have the ability to assess and understand individual impairments, to be able to explain necessary modifications in teaching sequences and/or methods to the staff, and to help establish rapport with the students.

4. Be able to establish a climate of empathy rather than sympathy with the students.

5. Be prepared and able to prepare the staff for a sustained long-range program since success may and often does come early although overall progress will generally be slow--
   patience is a prime requisite.

6. Realize the necessity for a continuing in-service training program for himself and his staff.

7. Possess imagination, originality, and creativity.

8. Feel he is one of a team of community level specialists working to improve the functional level of the retardate.

The volunteer or aide should--

1. Have as much swimming background and experience as possible.

2. Have the ability to understand the problems of retardation and to accept and respect the retardate as one of worth and dignity who can and should be helped.

3. Be able to establish rapport with the retarded individually and collectively.

4. Have the ability to carry out a planned program of instruction.

5. Be willing to stay with a long-range program realizing progress will often be very slow.

6. Be willing to participate in continuing in-service programs to improve his knowledge of mental retardation and his skill and competency in working with the retarded in swimming programs.

7. Have the imagination to be creative, the flexibility to make changes in approaches to meet the needs of individual students, the courage of his convictions and willingness to try something new, and the intelligence to make additional changes when he finds something is not working.

ORGANIZING AND ADMINISTERING THE PROGRAM

Many activities must be included in the complete instructional swim program for the mentally retarded -- shallow water experiences in a wading pool, individualized attention, and group instruction. *Activity Therapy Section, Rehabilitation Services, Pacific State Hospital, Pomona, California.*

Meticulous planning based on complete identification and careful analysis of many organizational and administrative problems and details is necessary if a program of swimming instruction for the mentally retarded is to be successful. No detail can be overlooked or left to chance--every aspect of this program must be planned and the plan expertly carried out. When swimming programs for the mentally retarded are being organized and administered, many varied factors must be considered: determining the need; involving all appropriate agencies, groups, and organizations in the community; recruiting and training instructors, aides, and volunteers; obtaining use of and constructing pool facilities; working with parents; handling emergency situations; developing and maintaining good public relations; obtaining necessary funds and finances; and developing an appropriate system of records and forms.

Determining The Need

Every effort should be made to include the mentally retarded in regular swimming programs where they are taught with the non-retarded. Realistically the retarded fall into several groups: those who can immediately be taught with the non-retarded, those who eventually will be able to be taught with the non-retarded, but now need special help and assistance (a half-way house approach), and those who according to best current assessments will never be able to be taught with the non-retarded because of physical, mental, social, or emotional deficits.

When instructional swimming programs for the mentally retarded are being organized and administered, the special, specific, and immediate needs of each of these groups must be carefully considered. Since special provisions and placements must be made in swimming programs for many retardates, the need for these programs must be determined through a thorough investigation of present programs in the community. To determine the feasibility of two or more communities working cooperatively in programs requiring special facilities like those needed for swimming, small and rural communities should investigate what nearby communities are doing.

Community Agencies and Organizations

Many different agencies and organizations are involved in programing for the mentally retarded and can be expected to assist in determining needs and to contribute in many ways to the success of the swimming program.

An organizational meeting should be called after initial contacts have been made with all groups. The purpose of the meeting is to acquaint these groups with the proposed program and to request their cooperation. Each agency might be asked to accept these assignments and responsibilities:

American Red Cross--to provide trained instructor personnel, instructor and administrative aides, locker room assistants, and qualified first aiders. Some chapters provide first aid supplies and equipment along with a physician from their First Aid Committee. Additionally, some local chapters provide transportation, printed charts and forms, promotional aids, and instructional audiovisual materials.

State and/or Local Associations for Retarded Children--to serve as a referral group, primary source for disseminating information about the program, and supplier of students. Personal contacts, telephone calls, mailings, and all other appropriate methods should be used to promote and advertise the swimming program with these groups.

Parent-Teachers' Associations--to assist with publicity, promotion, finances, recruitment, and transportation.

State and/or Local Medical Society--to advise and consult about activity restrictions for students with limiting physical defects and serious medical conditions.

Facility Managers and/or Owners--to provide use of pools for instructional and recreational swimming programs for the mentally retarded. Potential swimming sites include YMCA's, YWCA's, YMHA's, YWHA's, Boys' Clubs, public facilities, recreation departments, clubs, back yards, public schools, colleges, camps, lakes, and beaches.

United Fund--to serve as a liaison with participating agencies and to assist in interpreting how agencies can help or contribute to the program. Representatives of agencies can explain to all concerned the contributions made by each group receiving financial support from the United Fund.

Service and Civic Clubs (e.g., Civitan, Jaycees, Kiwanis, Rotary, Lions, Optimist, Elks)--to provide financial help (e.g., expense for stationery, printing, postage, equipment, supplies, pool rental, transportation), assistance in recruiting, and help with publicity. Members of some groups serve as instructors, aides, or volunteers; others assist with transportation by contacting car dealers and agencies to lend cars, station wagons, and busses for use in the program.

Public Information Agencies and Bureaus--to contact all news media (e.g., newspapers, magazines, radio stations, television channels) for assistance in recruiting students and instructors, and for interpreting and advertising the program.

Other Community Organizations and Institutions (e.g., YMCA's YWCA's, YMHA's, YWHA's, Boy Scouts, Girl Scouts, Camp Fire Girls, Recreation and Park Departments, Special Education Groups, Churches, Labor Unions, Physical Education Groups, Residential Facilities, Day Care Centers, Professional Organizations)--to assist in various ways which are in accordance with the structure, function, and role of the organization (i.e., provide instructor and aide personnel, manpower for administration and other needed services, transportation, and financial aid). Alpha Phi Omega, National College Fraternity affiliated with the Boy Scouts, sponsors programs, works directly with the mentally retarded, and helps scouting units provide more meaningful programs for the mentally retarded.

Training Instructors, Aides, and Volunteers

The success of any instructional swimming program for the mentally retarded is directly proportional to the dedication and ability of the staff. Basic to good swimming instruction is a staff which understands children, youth, and adolescents. Instructors must have capacity for empathy with the mentally retarded and multiply handicapped. Enthusiasm, initiative, imagination, patience, and the ability to analyze movements, especially those involved in swimming are also indispensable. Those who teach the mentally retarded to swim must be competent and skilled in swimming and aquatic activities, know sequences and progressions, and be open-minded and flexible. Instructors and aides should be carefully screened before being accepted into the program. Each should have on file an application which includes information about his background, experience, and training in swimming and aquatics and with the mentally retarded. A sample application form is included at the end of this Chapter.

Instructor and aide training programs should focus on activities, methods, and techniques--the what and how--and include enough of the rationale--the why--to provide sufficient background so programs can be flexible and better prepared to meet each student's needs. Many organizations and agencies provide training for swimming instructors and aides; some offer special courses; others include additional sessions in regular courses to prepare instructors and aides to work with the handicapped in general and the mentally retarded in particular. Among the organizations and agencies training instructors and aides to teach the mentally retarded to swim are:

American National Red Cross--water safety instructor rating may be obtained through local chapters or at national aquatic schools. Other courses include water safety instructor review, aquatic instructors of the handicapped, life saving, and small craft instruction.

Young Mens' Christian Association--leader training in aquatics may be obtained through local and area Y's.

Colleges and Universities--students may take courses in advanced swimming and aquatics which, when supplemented with information about the handicapped and retarded, may qualify them as instructors or aides to teach the retarded.

Even the best of courses and training programs must be supplemented by conferences and staff meetings involving auxiliary specialists--physicians, psychologists, psychiatrists, mental health personnel, occupational therapists, physical therapists, social workers, special educators, physical educators, and recreation personnel. Basic training in swimming and aquatics and appropriate knowledge of and experience with the retarded are needed by all instructors and aides working in the program.

The *complete* instructor must also be concerned with pool operation, first aid procedures, emergency drills, life-saving techniques, sanitation procedures, and parent-community relations. In addition to formal training programs, workshops and institutes or clinics should be planned to deal with special problems and other topics of concern to the staff.

Since it is desirable to have one-to-one personal supervision until retarded students learn basic water safety skills, competent and well-trained aides and volunteers are indispensible; their training programs must be well planned. Many American Red Cross chapters offer water safety aide-training for aquatics and courses for swimming aides. Many instructors find it necessary to train aides and volunteers so they can focus on the unique needs of their situation and on the students in their own program. Since aides are responsible to the instructor and work under his direct supervision, those who conduct their own training programs find such an approach helpful, productive and effective. Information sheets for aides, volunteers and assistants are helpful in providing data about general procedures and outlining specific techniques to use with the students. A sample information sheet is included at the end of this Chapter with other forms and records.

Instructors and aides can be given more time to work with students in the pool by using assistants for certain routine jobs and for some supervisory tasks. Generally assistants have duties and responsibilities in locker rooms, lavatories and shower rooms, and help students who need assistance to and from the pool area. Some assistants may be assigned to the pool area and help in the instructional program--this depends upon the needs of the program, and the interest, skills, and competencies of the assistants. Most assistants need some training in handling and lifting students and in helping them with braces and prosthetic devices; the chief instructor, therapist, doctor, parent, or the student himself may instruct assistants in these areas.

An on-going dynamic in-service training program must be held regularly if instructors and aides are to keep up with current trends, learn new and challenging activities and methods, and have questions answered. The complete in-service program consists of many different approaches and activities--

Instructor Reviews--offer opportunities to review and update basic swimming skills and teaching techniques; some focus on adapting and modifying techniques and approaches for the mentally retarded.

Workshops--provide short term programs to review skills, methods, techniques, and approaches and to discuss any material pertinent to the program or the mentally retarded. Workshops may include demonstration sessions with retarded children or participation sessions in which instructors and aides play the role of retarded students.

Staff Meetings--include periodic meetings for interchange among specialists involved in various parts of the program. Instructor-aide-assistant meetings are particularly valuable for exchanging information about the progress and behavior of students. Specialists and auxiliary personnel should be called in for assistance and guidance in dealing with students who have special problems.

Conferences--attend special programs on selected aspects of teaching the mentally retarded to swim; such sessions are included in some general programs dealing with physical education and recreation for the mentally retarded. Encourage instructors and aides to attend conferences and to exchange ideas with others teaching the mentally retarded to swim. A mutual attack upon common problems is only possible through sharing ideas and letting others benefit from similar experiences.

Audiovisual Materials (single pictures, sequence photographs, slides, films, single concept loop films, film strips, videotapes, phonograph records)--help to develop better understanding of swimming and aquatic activities, methods, techniques, and progressions.

Written Materials (magazines, newspapers, professional periodicals, pamphlets, books, newsletters, monographs, and other appropriate sources)--provide additional information about activities, methods, techniques, approaches, and adaptations which have been used successfully.

Instructors, aides, and assistants need to review constantly emergency drills and procedures in preparation for any eventuality in the pool, locker room, shower room, or while students are in transit to and from the pool area.

Parent Education and Awareness

The wholehearted understanding, support, enthusiasm, and involvement of parents must be obtained if aquatic programs for the mentally retarded are to be successful. Parents must accept that their youngster is mentally retarded, that he can be a contributing member of society, and that he can take part in community activities. Parents should be made aware of how swimming contributes to the mental, physical, social, and emotional adjustment of the mentally retarded. As parents become objective about the values of swimming, become aware of their child's newly learned skills, and recognize the need to encourage him to make use of these skills, they should be encouraged to provide more opportunities for the retardate to be included in family swim activities.

12

Solicit the parents' assistance--get them active in the program helping with public relations, fund raising, transportation, locker room assistance, and even in the pool teaching--preferably children other than their own. A well planned and organized program requires many telephone calls and personal contacts to explain the importance of the program and to get this kind of participation from parents.

Public Relations

All citizens in a community should be made aware of the need and importance of aquatic programs for the mentally retarded through an effective and on-going public relations and information program. Interaction among all concerned community agencies and good rapport among all involved in the program are basic to the success of any public relations efforts. The medical profession and persons from allied medical areas should be contacted personally to make sure they are aware of this program and of the importance of their professional support. These specialists can assist by preparing reports and making recommendations about intensity and level of activity permissible for those who seek permission to participate in the swimming program. Complete and constant community involvement is necessary to maintain an on-going instructional swimming program for the mentally retarded.

Records and Forms[1]

Sound administrative practice requires development and use of appropriate records and forms in instructional swimming programs for the mentally retarded. Records and forms *must* serve a purpose, not simply fill file cabinets and gather dust! Every bit of information obtained should help instructors better understand their students and should be valuable to instructors in planning and conducting a meaningful program for each student. Records and forms cannot simply be taken from other programs, agencies, or communities where similar programs exist; they must be based on the unique needs and special characteristics of the program and of the community in which they are to be used. Careful thought must be given the wording of records and forms since specialists with diverse backgrounds from various disciplines will use them. Terms have different meanings and are used for specific purposes by various specialists; therefore all words which may be confusing and create problems on the record form or in special instructions must be clearly defined. Every effort must be made to minimize or even eliminate trouble spots and semantic problems.

---

[1]Sample forms which have been used successfully in a variety of programs are found at the end of this Chapter.

Basic records and forms for swimming programs for the mentally retarded include:

Application Form

The sponsoring agency or organization should obtain an application form for each potential participant. Included on or with this form should be selected information about the organization and administration of the program, admission criteria, information about its overall operation, data about transportation, and the role of parents. Waiver and release forms giving permission to photograph the student and for his name to be included in publicity releases about the program should be included or attached to the application. No application waiver form or release should be considered complete without the signature of the student's parent or guardian.

Medical Evaluation

No one should be allowed to take part in vigorous physical activities, including swimming, without first having a thorough medical examination. The report of this examination should include pertinent facts from the health history of the student. It should provide information about any limiting conditions, particularly epilepsy, diabetes, asthma, and cardiac conditions; instructors must have information about students' physical limitations. Medical evaluation forms should be designed so swimming instructors can understand the information and apply it as a basis for selecting appropriate activities for the student. Special notations about activities related to the swimming program itself may be included—information about the student's ability to shower, dress and undress himself; body movements to be minimized or eliminated; intensity of activity permitted; therapeutic recommendations; and medications and their effects upon the student. Minimum medical information available to the instructor needs to include the diagnosis, special precautions necessary for the student, and similar pertinent facts in terms that can be understood and translated to action by the staff.

Detailed emergency information from the medical evaluation form must be readily accessible and actually kept at the swimming site. Emergency information should include how and where to contact the parents or guardian and the family doctor; names, addresses, and telephone numbers of two or three friends, neighbors, or relatives to contact in case parents, guardian or physician cannot be reached; a hospital preference in case of extreme emergency if none of those listed can be contacted. Other necessary information should be included—medications and special problems.

Personal History

If swimming programs are to make maximum contributions to the growth and development of the mentally retarded, instructions need to have pertinent information from the student's personal history. This is necessary to understand and appreciate the unique behavior and problems of each student and to assess reasons why he acts, reacts, and interacts as he does. The personal history should include information about the social, emotional, intellectual, physical and ethical makeup of the student; anecdotal entries and narrative reports provide background information to help explain the actions and re-actions of students. Parents, teachers, aides, professionals, and the student's peers can all provide helpful information although most data for the personal history form come from the student and his parents. Information about and examples of the student's behavior, data about his special interests and abilities, and a summary of minimum medical information (if it is not included in the medical evaluation) are especially helpful to the instructor for diagnosis, evaluation, and planning.

Instructors must guard against being unduly and adversely influenced by information from the personal history. Some instructors prefer *not* to review personal history forms until they actually meet and work with students a few times so they can make their own judgments; consequently, extremely glowing or negative reports do not influence or color an instructor's initial re-lationship with a student. Only after making their own determination about a student do these instructors review records to broaden knowledge about and understanding of the student.

Other instructors prefer to review all available information about stu-dents before they actually meet and work with them. These instructors feel they get to know students more quickly, and consequently can provide in-struction designed to meet the student's needs early in the program.

Some outstanding instructors use both of these approaches according to the situation and their students--their age, ability, and level of retardation. Regardless of the approach used, the good instructor--the one who understands his students and recognizes them as individuals of worth and dignity--knows individuals grow, develop, and change; he uses information and reports from the past to help him understand the student and his current behavior. This information must be considered as strictly confidential and can be used by the instructor only as a means of better understanding his students.

Reports to Parents

Opinions vary concerning the propriety of reporting certain kinds of in-formation to parents, particularly if this notes behavioral problems of the student and is done through the referral agency. Parents deserve and need to know of the growth and progress of their children; appropriate dialogue between staff and parents is necessary to gain their understanding of and support for the program. Much of the information contained in reports to parents neces-sarily focuses on development of and progress in attaining swimming skills; some provision should be made to report emotional and social progress.

Simple reporting systems can be devised to reflect changes in attitudes, effort, cooperation, stick-to-itiveness, and similar psychological, emotional, and social traits. Consideration should be given to periodic parent-instructor conferences; these are not difficult to organize and conduct. The values and benefits of these conferences are great for all concerned with the program and the student--the student, instructor, aide, and parent. Few agencies and organizations sponsoring swimming programs for the mentally retarded have fully used conferences as devices for upgrading their programs; the full impact of conferences upon programs has not been realized. Exploration and experimentation are needed to determine how reports to parents and parent-instructor conferences can most effectively contribute to the overall growth of these students and can contribute to their acquiring swimming and aquatic skills.

Swimming Skills and Progression Records or Check Lists

Forms and records to report progress in developing swimming skills are vital to the success of the instructional swimming program; these are important to instructors for making each lesson challenging; to the students for motivation; and to parents for seeing growth and progress in their child. These records should be designed according to sequences and progressions followed in teaching individual students and particular classes; they should be meaningful, functional, and significant to the student, and tell a story to all who see and use them. Many different forms have been devised and used successfully in swimming programs for the retarded--instructors can profit from and be guided by these approaches as they develop records or check lists for their programs. Some instructors use simple check lists; others have complex and comprehensive forms. In some systems any semblance of performing the skill warrants check-off and credit; in others a quantitative assessment--numerical weighting--is made for each skill; in some elaborate systems, graphs, pictures, cartoons, or other visual devices are used. Some ways to differentiate effort and attitude may be helpful:

    0 - no effort; wouldn't try
    T - tried--failed--quit
   TT - tried--failed--tried--quit
  TTT - tried continuously--failed continuously--had to be stopped

Daily records and reports of student progress can be used as a basis for planning instructional sessions and for making needed program changes. Swimming skills and progression records or check lists are among the most important of all records to instructors, aides, and others involved in the actual instruction.

Daily Progress and Attendance Forms

Some instructors adapt information from swimming skills and progression records or check lists to keep each student's daily progress and attendance. Accurate information about each student's progress gives the instructional staff direction and reason to adjust and modify the program to meet individual needs. Information about progress in attaining swimming skills, notes about student behavior, comments about relationships with peers, instructors, aides, and assistants, and specific anecdotes help the staff understand the student as an individual. Daily progress and attendance forms should be designed so that those filling in information and using them can do so easily.

16

Motivation Chart

A large, simple, colorful, and visible motivation chart can indicate student progress, reflect current status, and list awards received. Community and student individuality must be considered in developing motivation charts; what will work and be successful in one situation will fail miserably in another. Bright colors, pictures, and clever names can be incorporated effectively into motivation devices. Mentally retarded, especially EMR students, are usually highly motivated by methods and approaches which bring them personal recognition given by the instructional staff. Motivation charts and procedures should provide another way to offer and focus on increasingly greater challenges for students.

Accident Forms

An appropriate and adequate system of reporting accidents helps combat accidents, deals with emergency situations, and promotes greater safety consciousness among all involved in swimming and aquatic programs for the mentally retarded. Accident forms are necessary for the safety and protection, good and welfare of all connected with the program--students, instructors, parents, aides, and assistants. A complete reporting system is valuable in minimizing or eliminating situations and conditions which contribute to safety hazards and to accidents and in protecting the staff in the event of legal repercussions. All necessary and pertinent information should be included on the accident form; it should be filled out and filed with all persons or agencies requiring copies as soon after the accident as possible. Use of different colors to facilitate routing is suggested when multiple copies are needed; self-carbon or reproducing paper is also recommended.

First Aid and Emergency Procedures

First aid supplies must be adequate and readily accessible for immediate use in any part of the pool complex; emergency first aid equipment--stretcher, blanket, and a small kit--should be portable. All personnel--instructors, aides, assistants, and volunteers--involved in the program need basic first aid knowledge and training--Red Cross Standard or Advanced Courses, Boy or Girl Scout training, and Mini-Rescue Courses provide the basic knowledge and skills to prepare personnel. Addresses and telephone numbers of emergency rescue squads, hospitals, clinics, and doctors, and a card file giving all necessary emergency information for participants in the program should be readily available at the swimming site. Special information and notations about students with seizures and about procedures to handle these students should be included with the information on file at the swimming site; instructors, aides, and assistants need to be trained to handle these cases.

Standard first aid and emergency procedures should be established according to the type of facility and ways suggested for handling the rest of a class while first aid care is being administered. Particular techniques should be worked out and used until a person injured in the water can be taken to shallow water or placed on shore or the deck of the pool with minimum distraction.

Periodic drills should be a part of staff training--initial and in-service--and include all instructors, aides, and assistants. Practice and drills should focus on the unique features of the pool, beach, or water site used for the program and occasionally involve the unexpected--surprise drowning, fire in the locker room with a blocked exit, seizure, multiple drowning, and similar situations.

Swimming safety standards for the mentally retarded include the same basic precautions as those taken in instructing physically and mentally normal students. Generally, safety standards and emergency procedures for small craft instruction should be the same as those followed in usual *novice* groups and should include swim qualifications and over-the-side tests. Special procedures and precautions should be taken so students can avoid being chilled. Students should avoid excessive *in-and-out* procedures and should dry off immediately when getting out of the water to stay.

First Aid Procedures for Convulsive Disorders
(Handling Seizures in the Water)

Panic, fear, excitement, or over-exertion may cause or *trigger* a seizure in a person who has a convulsive disorder.[2] All staff members should be well versed in procedures to follow with seizure cases before, during, and after actual attacks in the water.

1. Instructors should verify that medication has been taken as scheduled when medication has been indicated on the medical or personal history record.

2. A competent swimmer should be within reach or nearby at all times the seizure-prone student is in the water. To insure

---

[2]By reference to convulsive disorders is meant grand mal, petit mal, psychomotor disorders, etc. In many individuals, seizures tend to occur mainly during sleep and periods of relative inactivity; they are less apt to occur during periods of physical and mental exertion. Three decisive factors must be considered in arriving at a reliable judgment about active participation: (a) whether good control of the condition is maintained by medication, (b) whether the extent and intensity of participation poses a significant threat to the individual's physical condition, and (c) whether the individual is co-operative and in control of any impulsiveness. "Convulsive Disorders and Participation in Sports and Physical Education," *Journal of the American Medical Association*, November 4, 1968 (Vol. 206, No. 6).

prompt assistance if an attack occurs in the water, full use should be made of the *Buddy System* so at least one individual student or adult will be responsible for and able to give immediate aid. These individuals should be given procedures to follow with the seizure student in the water. Generally the student experiencing the seizure can do less damage to himself if he is kept in the water until the active seizure stage has passed. Instructors and aides should be oriented to continue regular activities and keep students away from the seizure victim during the attack and while he is being removed from the water. Students with convulsive disorders may be identified when in the water by having them wear different colored bathing caps or suits.

3. Some who suffer from convulsive disorders may recognize an aura just prior to the onset of a seizure and should be encouraged to alert the instructor of the impending attack.

4. Students who suffer seizures in the water should be supported with the face up and out of the water, until the seizure has passed. Rescuers should use a chin pull position with the victim's head close to the rescuer's shoulder so as to maintain an open airway while proceeding to the nearest stationary support. Students should not be restrained during seizures.

5. Students should be removed from the area, with a minimum of distraction and taken to the first aid room or a quiet area as soon as recovery from the active seizure stage is apparent.

6. Instructors should arrange a conference with the student's parents and family physician after the first seizure to arrive at a standard procedure to follow in case of subsequent seizures.

7. Blankets and a litter should be kept at the swimming site.

8. Standard first aid procedures for seizure causes should be followed once the student is out of the water and on the deck or shore.

9. The family physician should be called immediately if convulsions reoccur during the same instructional period-- in all cases, parents should be notified.

Information To Be Kept At Pool Site

Patient Swimming Approved PACIFIC STATE HOSPITAL	NAME _____ AGE _____
Approved for: _____ Swimming Pool _____ Wading Pool <u>Physical Limitations</u>: _____ Ambulation _____ Vision _____ Hearing _____ Arm Movement _____ Cardiac	_____ I.Q. _____ P.Q. Epileptic: _____ Yes _____ No Type of Seizure: _____ Frequency: _____
APPROVALS: _____ Ward Physician	DATE: _____ _____ Area Supervisor

' ' ' first three	RECREATION CENTER FOR THE HANDICAPPED,INC
' ' ' letters in	Student's Information Card
' ' ' last name	

STUDENT'S NAME: _____ AGE___ DATE OF ENROLLMENT____
HOME ADDRESS: _____ TELEPHONE: _____
ORGANIZATION REFERRING PARTICIPANT: _____
MEDICAL DIAGNOSIS _____ DESCRIPTION_____
PART OF BODY INVOLVED: Right Arm:___ Left Arm:___ Neck:____
Right Leg:___ Left Leg:___ Trunk:___ Other:____
PHYSICIAN'S RECOMMENDATIONS: Nose Clips:___ Ear Plugs___ Dive___
SHOULD NOT PUT FACE UNDER WATER___ SPECIFIED BODY POSITIONS____
BODY POSITIONS CONTRADICTED: _____
SPECIFIC MOVEMENTS OR ACTIONS_____ OTHER___
PHYSICIAN'S NAME_____ TELEPHONE___
INSTRUCTOR'S NAME_____ GROUP___
FLOTATION DEVICE RECOMMENDATION_____ DATE___

Medical And Personal History Records

RECREATION CENTER FOR THE HANDICAPPED, INC.
Fleishhacker Pool Building
Great Highway near Sloat Boulevard
San Francisco, California   94132

NAME:_____ AGE:_____
HOME ADDRESS:_____ TELEPHONE:_____
NAME OF PARENT OR GUARDIAN:_____
ORGANIZATION REFERRING PARTICIPANT:_____

PHYSICIAN'S RECOMMENDATION FOR AQUATIC PARTICIPATION

The above named person is planning to enroll in the Aquatic Program of the Recreation Center for the Handicapped, in cooperation with the Aquatics Division
of the S.F. Recreation & Park Department. The program includes recreational
water games and sports in addition to the instructional program. This recommendation will assist in the proper group placement of the participant and in
the selection of appropriate swimming strokes and body positions, if any. Your
assistance in this matter will be greatly appreciated.

1. Medical Diagnosis:_____

2. Diagnosis in Laymen's Terms:_____

3. Parts of the body involved (if any). Please indicate degree:
    (Slight, Moderate, Severe).

    Arm - Right:_____ Leg - Right:_____
    Arm - Left:_____ Leg - Left:_____
    Neck:_____ Trunk:_____
    Other:_____

4. Applicant (please check):
    needs to wear a nose clip_____ear plugs_____should not dive_____
    should not put face under water_____. Any other specific precautions
    which should be taken? List:_____

    _____

5. Do you recommend any specific body position?
    Back_____ Left Side_____
    Stomach_____ Right Side_____

6. Do you recommend any specific movements or actions?

    _____

7. Other Comments:_____

    _____
    I hereby (give/do not give) my approval for the above named person
    to engage in this Recreational Aquatic Program.

Date:_____   Name of Physician:_____

                                            Phone:_____

Announcement and Application

RECREATION CENTER FOR THE HANDICAPPED, INC.
Fleishhacker Pool Building
Great Highway near Sloat Boulevard
San Francisco, California   94132

Are you interested in having fun - meeting people -- learning new skills - playing water games? The way to do all these things is join the Center's Aquatic Program.

The Aquatic Program offers recreation and instruction in swimming skills for all ages. Swimmers are divided into two groups:

     ADULTS - Balboa Pool, Thursday, 5:00 - 7:00 p.m.

     CHILDREN & TEENS - Hamilton Pool, Friday, 4:00 - 6:00 p.m.

Please bring your own labeled suit, cap, and towel if possible. An after - swimming snack is provided by the Center.

If you are interested, please complete the attached application as soon as possible and return it to the Center. A medical form will be sent to your doctor for completion before your application can be accepted.

If you are now a member of the Aquatic Program, please fill out the application as we are interested in bringing present files up-to-date.

Hope to hear from you soon.

                                        Sincerely,

                                        Miss Kristin Ives
                                        Aquatic Specialist

RECREATION CENTER FOR THE HANDICAPPED, INC.
Fleishhacker Pool Building
Great Highway near Sloat Boulevard
San Francisco, California   94132

CHILD_____

TEEN_____

ADULT_____

NAME_____ AGE_____

ADDRESS_____ PHONE_____

PARENT/GUARDIAN_____

HANDICAP_____ HEIGHT_____

Please check if used:

Braces:_____   Can walk some:_____
Crutches:_____   Can dress self:_____
Wheel Chair:_____   Needs aid in dressing:___

Swimming Experience:

Has applicant ever been in water?   Yes_____No_____

Has applicant ever been in deep water? Yes_____No_____

Does applicant have any fear of the water? Yes_____No_____

Can applicant swim and to what extent?_____

Have you any helpful suggestions that you would care to make in order to help the instructor work with your child?_____

Can you provide transportation to pool? Yes_____No_____

Can you provide transportation to home? Yes_____No_____

IN CASE OF EMERGENCY:

Name_____   Doctor_____

Address_____   Address_____

Phone_____   Phone_____

Please enroll____ (applicant)_____in the Aquatic program. We realize that regularity in attendance is important and will make an effort to have applicant attend every class. Applicant has my permission to participate in all Aquatic activities except for those restrictions indicated on physician's recommendation.

DATE_____   SIGNATURE_____

APPLICATION FOR ADULT AND CHILDREN'S HANDICAPPED
SWIMMING PROGRAM

NAME_____ AGE_____ BIRTH DATE_____

ADDRESS_____ PHONE_____

OCCUPATION_____

TYPE OF PHYSICAL DIFFICULTY_____

_____

EXTENT OF PHYSICAL DIFFICULTY_____

_____

SWIMMING ABILITY AND EXPERIENCE_____

WILL HELP BE NEEDED IN LOCKER ROOM IN DRESSING_____

CAPABLE OF TAKING A SHOWER_____HELP IS NEEDED_____

FAMILY DOCTOR_____

ANY COMMENTS_____

_____

WAIVER AND RELEASE STATEMENT

We, or I, hereby, for ourselves, or myself, or my heirs, executors and administrators, waive and release any and all right and claims for damages we, or I, may have against the Longview YMCA, their agents, representatives, successors, and assigns for any and all injuries suffered by the undersigned during this program.

_____

(Participant's Signature)

This along with the
Doctor's form must be
completed and returned
to the YMCA

_____

(Parent's signature if under 21)

DATE_____

24

APPLICATION FOR ADMISSION INTO SWIMMING CLASS

FOR MENTALLY RETARDED CHILDREN

Name of Applicant_____Age_____

Home Address_____Phone_____

Is Your Child Attending School?_____If so, where?_____

Has your child ever been in the water?_____Where? Pool_____Beach_____

Does your child have any fear of the water?_____

Does your child swim and to what extent?_____

                     Deep water?_____

Has your child ever been in a swimming class?_____

Does your child respond to orders?_____

Does your child have a hearing defect?_____

Is your child able to speak?_____

Have you any helpful suggestions that you would care to make in order to help the instructor work with your child?

_____

_____

_____

                           _____
                           Signature of Parent or Guardian

                           _____
                                   Address

                           _____
                                   Phone

Kanawha-Clay Chapter, American Red Cross
Charleston, West Virginia

APPLICATION FOR ADMISSION INTO THE ADULT AND
CHILDREN'S HANDICAPPED SWIMMING PROGRAM

Student's Name _____   Birth   Home Address _____
                                          Date

Name of Parent or Guardian _____   Telephone Number _____

Organization referring student _____

The following information is to be provided by a physician:

In order that the specific needs of the applicant can be met, please provide the following information.

1. Physician's diagnosis including affected parts of the body_____

_____

_____

2. Particular body movements permitted and not permitted

_____

_____

_____

3. State precautions that should be taken

_____

_____

4. Range of motion: Limited 0-33%; Moderate 34-66%; Maximum 67-100%

_____

_____

Date_____   Name of Physician_____

Continued on next page

26

(Confidential material for retarded or emotionally disturbed classes)

NAME _____

ADDRESS _____ PHONE _____

BIRTH DATE _____ IQ _____

DATE _____ C.A.* _____ M.A.** _____ APPROX. GRADE _____

DATE _____ C.A. _____ M.A. _____ APPROX. GRADE _____

DATE _____ C.A. _____ M.A. _____ APPROX. GRADE _____

Family Background: (Include child's present adjustment in the family)

Cooperation with adults:

Social Maturity: (Include getting along with other children)

Physical development and coordination:

Medical, mental, neurological problems:

Attention span and ability to concentrate:

Pupil's interests:

* Chronological age
** Mental age

YOUNG MEN'S CHRISTIAN ASSOCIATION
Longview, Washington

Permission Slips

RECREATION CENTER FOR THE HANDICAPPED, INC.
Fleishhacker Pool Building
Great Highway near Sloat Boulevard
San Francisco, California   94132

PERMISSION SLIP

_____has my permission to attend

the Recreation Center for the Handicapped, Inc. Program on the

following days: THURSDAY EVENING TEEN PROGRAM_____

                       FRIDAY SWIMMING PROGRAM _____

It is my understanding that the Center's bus will pick up my

child at _____ and will take

him to the planned program for that day.

Date_____   Parent_____

                         Program Coordinator_____

                         School Principal_____

28

September, 1967

Dear Parents:

The Ashtabula County Child Welfare Board and the Ashtabula YM-YWCA are sponsoring a swimming program for the children attending Happy Hearts School.

Parents are required to furnish swimming suits and towels. Students should bring these prior to September 11, 1967, the first day of swimming.

In order for your child to participate in the swimming program, we will need a signed permission as indicated below.

DO NOT DETACH - Please return to Happy Hearts School before September 8.

I give permission to the Ashtabula County Child Welfare Board, Happy Hearts School and the Ashtabula YM-YWCA for my child:

_____
(Child's Name)

to participate in the swimming program.

(Check one)   Yes_____

No_____

Signed:_____
(Parent or Guardian)

PLEASE NOTE: Do not forget to send a towel with your child

and PLEASE have it marked in some way with his or her name.

Ashtabula County Child Welfare Board
HAPPY HEARTS SCHOOL
2036 East Prospect Road
Ashtabula, Ohio
Telephone 997-3412

March 29, 1967

Dear Parents:

As you know, we are making plans for the April "Swim Show" that will be coming up on Friday, April 21. The program will be held at the YM-YWCA.

In order to plan effectively for this program, it will be necessary to know at this time whether or not you plan to have your son/daughter participate in the show. The program is scheduled to start at 7:00 p.m. It would be necessary for you to have your child at the "Y" no later than 6:30 p.m. which means if you are planning to allow your child to participate, it will be necessary for you to provide transportation to and from the "Y."

Will you please fill in the bottom portion of this letter and return it to the school as quickly as possible.

Thank you for your cooperation.

Sincerely,

HAPPY HEARTS SCHOOL

_____
Wayne G. Reese
Director

WGR:cjm

I give permission for my son/daughter_____to participate
                                           (Name of Child)
in the April Swim Show:
                                        _____ _____
                                         Yes   No

I will see to it that transportation is arranged for my child to attend
the show:
                                        _____ _____
                                         Yes   No

_____
(Signature of Parent or Guardian)

30

Daily Record Form

SWIMMING PROGRESS CHART

PUPIL'S NAME_____

INSTRUCTOR'S NAME_____

	Dates						Problems/Comments
Enter water							Date:
Walk through water							
Face In water							
Duck Head Under							
Pick up objects under water							Date:
Blowing Bubbles							
Bobbing							
Jelly Fish Float							
Jump into shallow water							Date:
Front float							
Back float							
Standing up from back							
Standing up from front							
Back tow							
Front tow							Date:
Back glide							
Front Glide							
Rolling over fr.to b.							
Rolling over b. to fr.							Date:
Flutter kick on back							
Finning on back							
Dog paddle on front							
Turning							
Tread water							
Swim 20' on back							Date:
Swim 20' on front and return							
Game							
Cooperation							Date:
Interest							

Comments

Kanawha-Clay Chapter, American Red Cross
Charleston, West Virginia

RECREATION CENTER FOR THE HANDICAPPED, INC.
Fleishhacker Pool Building
Great Highway near Sloat Boulevard
San Francisco, California   94132

PARTICIPANT'S PROGRESS REPORT

(To be filled out by the Leader of the Group the
Participant is assigned to. This form should be
completed for each participant twice a year or
as requested.)

NAME_____AGE_____NATURE OF_____
                                                       HANDICAP

OBSERVATIONS:

    I.   SELF-CARE SKILLS:

   II.   SOCIAL SKILLS:

  III.   COMMUNICATION:

   IV.   RECREATION ACTIVITIES ENJOYED:

    V.   SPECIAL QUALITIES OR ATTRIBUTES:

   VI.   SPECIAL DIFFICULTIES:

  VII.   GROWTH:

 VIII.   GENERAL COMMENTS:

Signed_____

Date_____Title_____

32

FISH

		Camper's Name
		SURFACE DIVE IN CHEST DEEP WATER
		FLUTTER BACK SCULL
		RACING DIVE (DECK PLUNGE)
		VERTICAL SCULLING AND TREADING
		FLUTTER KICK ONE LENGTH
		CRAWL STROKE W/START AND TURN
		VERTICAL SCULLING HANDS ONLY
		PLAIN STANDING FRONT DIVE
		HORIZONTAL SCULLING
		SWIM 100 YDS. USING 2 STROKES
		CAMP PERIOD I II III IV ATTENDANCE

TADPOLE

		Camper's Name
		RIDE ON FRONT LOOK AT BOTTOM
		KICK TO WALL
		FRONT GLIDE & REGAIN FEET
		SITTING DIVE WITH GLIDE
		CRAWL STROKE
		ROTARY BREATHING
		BOBBING (RHYTHMIC BREATHING)
		BACK GLIDE
		RECOVER OBJECT
		FLUTTER KICK
		SWIM 25 FEET
		CAMP PERIOD I II III IV ATTENDANCE

MINNOW

		Camper's Name
		FLUTTER KICK WITH ROTARY BREATHING
		JUMPING SURFACE DIVES
		UNDERWATER SWIM
		SWIM 20 FEET
		RHYTHMIC ROTARY BREATHING
		SAFETY SWIM
		CHANGE TO RESTING STROKE
		COMBINATION SWIM IN DEEP WATER
		CAMP PERIOD I II III IV ATTENDANCE

FLYING FISH

Camper's Name		
UNDERWATER PUSH AND GLIDE		
SURFACE DIVES 6-10 Ft. DEEP		
CORKSCREW SWIM ONE LGTH.		
FROG KICK ONE LENGTH		
TREAD WATER 30 SECS.		
RUNNING JUMP FROM BOARD		
SWIM 100 YDS. CRAWL STROKE		
SIDESTROKE R AND L ONE LGTH.		
RUNNING FRONT BOARD DIVE		
SWIM 220 YDS. ANY STYLE		

ATTENDANCE CAMP PERIOD I II III IV

SHARK

Camper's Name		
BOB 20 TIMES AND FLOAT		
RUNNING PLUNGE FRONT BOARD		
BREAST STROKE W/START AND TURN		
BACK DIVE		
UNDERWATER SWIM 35 FT.		
BACK STROKE W/START AND TURN		
BACK JACKKNIFE DIVE		
LIFESAVING STROKE ONE LENGTH		
RUNNING FRONT ½ TWIST DIVE		
SWIM 440 YDS ANY STYLE		

ATTENDANCE CAMP PERIOD I II III IV

Wilmington YMCA, Delaware

In this report we wish to convey to you the extent to which your child has developed in swim skills. Also shown is the whole scope of the programme so you can see the direction in which we are moving.

#1. ACCOMMODATION TO WATER

Enter Water			
Walk Through Water			
Front and Back Tow			
Face In			
Duck Under			
Blow Bubbles – Hold Breath			
Bobbing			
Retrieve Object Underwater			

#2. BODY BUOYANCY

Flutter Board – Front Back			
Jelly Fish Float			
Turtle Tuck			
Front Float – Stand			
Front Glide			
Back Float – Stand			
Back Glide			
Roll Over – Front to Back			
Roll Over – Back to Front			

#3. MOVING THROUGH SHALLOW WATER

Front Glide and Flutter kick			
Front Glide – Kick and Stroke			
Back Glide and Kick			
Back Glide – Kick and Firm			
Dog Paddle			
Swim Distance on Front – Note Distance			
Swim Distance on Back – Note Distance			
Swim and Change Direction			
Swim and Change Position			

#4. CHEST DEEP WATER

Tread Water – Note Time			
Jump In – Level Out – Swim			
Dive from Deck – Swim			
Swim 30' on Front – Note Distance			
Swim 30' on Back – Note Distance			
Swim 30' on Front – Turn and Return – Note Distance			
Swim 30' Turn – Change Position			

#5. DEEP WATER

Water Entries			
Jump In			
Stride Jump			
Beginner Dive			
Standing Dive – Deck			
Standing Dive – Board			
Surface Dive			

#6. STROKES

Front Crawl – Note Distance			
Breast Stroke – Note Distance			
Side Stroke – Note Distance			
Elementary Back – Note Distance			
Back Crawl – Note Distance			
Swim on Front – 60' plus			
Swim on Back – 60' plus			

#7. WATER SAFETY PRACTICES

Tread Water 1 Minute plus			
Jelly Fish Float for Leg Cramp			
Swim Change Position			
Swim Change Direction			
Reaching Assists			
Pole, Paddle, Towel, Clothing			
Swim on Back – Arms only 35' plus			
Swim on Back – Legs only 35' plus			

For further explanation of skills, see back of CARC Swim Test Sheets and the Canadian Red Cross Society Water Safety Manual.

COMMENT:

Developed and Published by the CANADIAN ASSOCIATION FOR RETARDED CHILDREN in co-operation with the Water Safety Service of The Canadian Red Cross.

35

Name _____ Case _____ Ward _____

Wading Pool ____ Large Pool ____ Water Show Participant (Yes) ____ (No) ____

Participation Abilities	Good	Fair	Poor	General Comments & Recommendations
A. Ability to sustain effort				
B. Ability to follow directions				
C. Ability to assume responsibility				
D. Cooperative				
E. Performance				
1. Accuracy of work				
2. Quality of work				
3. Ability to work with group (contribution of group efforts)				
4. Adaptability (socially acceptable behavior)				
5. Is able to dress self				
6. Knows procedure of checking personal clothes				
F. Attendance				

SKILLS	Good	Fair	Poor	SKILLS	Good	Fair	Poor
TADPOLE (Beginner)				MINNOWS (Intermediate)			
Physical adjustment				Swimming in place			
Mental adjustment				Change positions			
Breath-holding				Elementary backstroke			
Rhythmic breathing				Diving			
Prone float & glide				Underwater			
Back float & glide				Use of life jacket			
Kick glide, front-back				Elementary rescues			
Armstroke				Treading			
Combined front stroke							
Combined back stroke				DOLPHINS (Swimmer)			
				Side stroke			
ADVANCED TADPOLE (Adv.Beg.)				Breast stroke			
Change of direction				Hand-over-hand			
Turning over				Sculling			
Leveling off				Turns			
Jump in waist deep				Surface dive			
Jump in deep water				Long shallow dive			
Plain front dive				Running dive			
Safety skills				Inverted scissors kick			
				Inverted breaststroke kick			
				5-minute swim			
				30-minute swim			

American Red Cross certificates	Date Received	Comments
1. Beginner	_____	
2. Advanced Beg.	_____	
3. Intermediate	_____	
4. Swimmer	_____	
5. Advanced Swm.	_____	
6. _____	_____	

RE 840 RE

(Signature) _____
Water Safety Instructor

RECREATION CENTER FOR THE HANDICAPPED, INC.
Fleishhacker Pool Building
Great Highway near Sloat Boulevard
San Francisco, California   94132

Date:_____

APPLICATION FOR PROGRAM LEADERSHIP

NAME:_____ AGE:_____ SEX:_____

ADDRESS:_____ PHONE:_____
       number   street   zone   city

Condition of health:_____Any physical handicaps?_____

Employer (if any):_____

School?_____Graduate?_____

    Year?_____Major?_____Minor_____

Previous Aquatic Experience: (indicate - paid/volunteer

._____
_____
_____

Certification (Please check and date)

First Aid_____Year_____

First Aid Instruction_____Year_____

Life Saving_____Year_____

Water Safety Instructor_____Year_____

Do you belong to an Aquatics Organization? If so, give:

Name_____Location_____

Position held_____

Can you teach or lead any of the following activities? Please check

    WATER GAMES_____WATER BALLET_____

    WATER POLO_____STUNTS_____

    DIVING_____OTHER(please list)_____
                                        _____
                                        _____

                                        Signed:_____

Interviewed by_____Assigned_____Date_____

YOUNG MEN'S CHRISTIAN ASSOCIATION

15th & Douglas   Longview, Wash.

EVALUATION SHEET FOR PUBLIC SCHOOL CHILDREN'S SPECIAL CLASSES

NAME_____DATE_____

FAMILY
What changes do you notice in health, appearance, and personality of the participant? Any comments or recommendations?_____

_____

CLASSROOM TEACHER
Did you notice any improvement in personality abnormalities of the child or any change in physical appearance?_____

_____

Have you noticed any change in study habits?_____

_____

SCHOOL PSYCHOLOGIST
Has there been any significant emotional improvement in the child?_____Does he function better with the group?_____Has he gained confidence and shown awareness in developing skills?_____

_____

PARTICIPANT
Has this swimming experience been enjoyable?_____ Why have you enjoyed this group experience?_____

_____

What physical improvements have you noted?_____

_____

INSTRUCTOR
How has the participant progressed with his swimming skills?_____

_____

To what degree has the participant progressed in his ability to adjust to group activities?_____

_____

Information Sheet For Instructors And Other Helpers In The Pool

1. Secure the child's records. Read them carefully each time you work with child. Do not let the child read the records if there is confidential information included.

2. Note especially if records indicate activities which should be eliminated: e.g., NO DIVING, NO JUMPING.

3. Return records before taking child in pool.

4. Be sure child has towel with him. Put towel somewhere close by so you can get it if he gets cold.

5. Take child out of pool as soon as you notice he is shivering. After he is warm again, return to pool.

6. At end of lesson: Go with child to locker room at the end of lesson. (Be sure he takes towel with him.) If someone is there to help him you need not stay but if no one in the locker room is able to help him, dress him and take him to person in charge of transportation.

7. Be sure to record student's progress after each lesson.

8. For further information on your pupil, see instructor to whom you are responsible.

To Locker Room Assistants

1. Be sure child knows where to find his clothes and braces so he can tell adult who helps him at close of class.

2. Be sure child has his towel when he goes to the pool. The instructor will see that he brings it back to the locker room after class.

3. Take child to the person responsible for him when he is ready to leave the locker room. Do not leave the child until he has been acknowledged by this person.

Kentucky Society for Crippled Children
Louisville, Kentucky

METHODS

Innovation, creativity, and originality are indispensible if instructors are to meet the needs of their students. Karen has fun in a towel hammock. *Bart Parker, Jacksonville, Florida*

Tradition and convention have too long dominated programs for the mentally retarded who have been directed and manipulated to fit preconceived molds. Retardates within given IQ--chronological age or mental age--chronological age categories have been assumed to function identically in all activities; a single program and standardized approaches appropriate for all retardates in a given group participating in a specific activity have been sought. Emphasis has been on using a retarded student's talent and skill to promote programs rather than using activities to contribute to the individual! There has been an increasing awareness of the importance of physical education and recreational activities in educating and training the mentally retarded, and for promoting their optimal growth and development. Many new physical education and recreation programs have been developed and numerous existing programs have been upgraded and enriched during the last several years. Similarly, personnel connected with aquatic programs for the retarded have been seeking appropriate materials and new approaches for their efforts on behalf of the mentally retarded.

By and large, mentally retarded have been taught swimming in conventional ways and in usual sequences found in swimming programs for the non-retarded. Many swimming programs have not met the needs of the retarded since they have been too advanced, progressed at rates too rapid, and included methods and approaches too abstract. Traditional programs have always been effective for some retardates and quite satisfactory for others after they develop certain basic skills and competencies. Unfortunately, many retardates have not responded or progressed when conventional approaches and usual sequences have been used; often this has added to their feelings of failure and frustration. There is a need for those who teach swimming to the mentally retarded to try new and innovative approaches and activities; many factors must be considered as aquatic programs for the retarded are developed, refined, and expanded. A number of these factors must be considered long before the student is brought to the swimming site.

Education of the Physical

Instructors of physical activity programs usually are concerned with *education through the physical*--use of a variety of physical activities to achieve selected physical, mental, emotional, social, and ethical objectives. Minimum levels of physical fitness and motor proficiency have been too often overlooked as important requisites for success in a variety of physical and recreational activities. *Education of the physical* must precede education through the physical. Minimum levels of strength, endurance, agility, balance, power, speed, flexibility, and coordination are essential to success in most physical activities. Complex motor activities also require an adequate base of such fundamental movements as crawling, creeping, walking, running, jumping, hopping, skipping, galloping, leaping, throwing, catching, pushing, and pulling. These elements of physical fitness and motor ability must not be overlooked if one is to be successful in learning to swim. Conversely, swimming itself can promote the development of these important physical and motor attributes.

Motor-Perceptual Considerations

Perceptual ability[1] is important to the attainment of motor skills and can develop along with them. However, perceptual development is often overlooked in teaching swimming. For example, some instructors have reported that swimmers rely upon true balance and internal righting mechanisms to gain and maintain buoyant positions in the water. In swimming the body is in a horizontal position, the eyes often closed or the vision restricted by the water, so that an individual with serious balance problems might be adversely affected in his ability to swim smoothly and efficiently.

---

[1] Perceptual ability as used in this publication is an awareness one has of his body and its orientation. It involves judgments related to time, space, shape, intensity, force, and balance. Activation of sense receptors, interpretation of stimuli, and use of previous experience are important in perception.

A variety of perceptual abilities must be considered as basic to learning most swimming strokes--the student must be able to distinguish right from
left, up from down, top from bottom, together from apart, in from out, and
front from back. While these might appear to be simple and obvious, they can
create problems for the individual who has not *learned* his body has two sides
which work together or independently, synchronized or in opposition. Swimming
instructors must realize an individual develops an internal awareness to distinguish between sides of his own body (laterality) before he can project this
relationship to objects in space away from his body (directionality) and gives
the sides labels--right-left-up-down-before-behind. Laterality precedes and
forms the base for directionality.

Since the majority of a swimmer's body is immersed in water, he has greater
stimulation of sensory nerve endings. This may have adverse effects on the
hyperactive who experiences greater stimulation than usual and may find it difficult to control a variety of movements which affect his efficiency in swimming. On the other hand water may stimulate the hypoactive and passive. Activity in water causes the individual to make adjustments according to forces from
the water on his body as well as from the force he generates against the water.

The Multi-Sensory Approach

Generally the greater the number of senses activated in teaching a skill
the faster and more permanent the learning. While many non-retarded rely primarily on the eyes for learning, some instructors report the retarded learn
more effectively and retain more through auditory channels. However, most
young and low level retardates respond best to visual stimuli since they
perform and learn from imitation. Extensive use of sensory and tactile stimulation has also been effective with young retardates and those of lower
functional levels. When two or more senses are used simultaneously learning
is reinforced, more rapid, and likely to be more permanent.

In teaching the retarded a systematic and progressive approach should
take into consideration five stimuli patterns:

1. *Assistive*--Guide body parts through desired movements to capi-
    talize on kinesthetic (proprieoceptive) feedback from muscles
    to the brain (the ability that lets us know where our body parts
    are or what they are doing when they are out of our field of
    vision). Guiding an individual's arms through proper movements
    and sequences in the crawl or moving a student's head properly
    in breathing are applications of this principle. Various
    mechanical devices can be developed by the creative instructor
    to capitalize upon this principal in meeting individual needs of
    students.

2. *Tactile*--Touch body parts so the student feels the part to
    be moved. Touching the arm to be moved or the leg to be kicked
    are simple examples of application. This is seldom if ever
    used by itself, but is a means of reinforcing visual and/or
    verbal stimuli.

42

3. *Visual stimulus*--Stimulate eyes through demonstrations, pictures, films, slides, single concept loops, television, or other visual stimuli. The student sees what he is to do and then imitates or reproduces the movements.

4. *Verbal stimulus*--Stimulate ears through the spoken word. The student is given oral instructions, commands, or problems to solve to which he must respond.

5. *Abstract stimulus*--Use various stimuli--signals, signs, words, numbers, colors, drum beats, or other signals. The student receives, interprets, and translates into action the stimuli.

In some instances instructors find it necessary to use one of these approaches at a time. If teaching a certain skill requires a concrete stimulus pattern--assistive or tactile--the same approach will probably be needed when the student moves to the next skill. Changing the level of stimuli introduces a new dimension and provides the retardate with more abstract, difficult, and challenging tasks. Progress can be assessed in this way and in moving to more advanced skills.

Cause and Effect Relationships

Frequently instructors fail to distinguish clearly between *cause and effect relationships* when a swimmer has difficulty with a particular skill, movement, or stroke. These instructors see only that a student does not go into the water, has difficulty with the flutter kick, or does not move through the water. Often the instructor focuses on what he sees--external symptoms--rather than determining the cause of the problem. If the instructor's approach works, the student progresses; if it doesn't work, the student plateaus and may even regress. Often approaches to determine why an individual is having difficulty are over-complicated.

Instructors must evaluate constantly to determine where the student is, to decide what are his immediate needs, and to direct him in challenging and meaningful activity. Every instructor should have an indelible visual image of the ideal way in which a movement, skill, or stroke should be performed and at the same time be sufficiently flexible to allow for individual differences. The good instructor never overlooks the obvious but is still alert for subtle causes and complex factors underlying problems. Generally, it is difficult to assess the cause of a problem from a single situation or observation--consistency in behavior patterns over a period of time provides insight, leads, and clues to causes of problems. Problems in learning to swim can come from what appear to be unrelated areas--poor motor function, inadequate levels of physical fitness, inappropriate perception, lack of understanding of instructions and of what is expected, lack of previous experience in related activities, lack of motivation, problems in communication or rapport between instructor and student, or inappropriate methods and activities. The instructor must not overlook visual evaluation, observation tempered with experience and common sense judgments to help determine cause and effect relationships.

Break Down Skills into Sequential Progressions

So often swimming instructors tend to teach as they were taught rather than as they were taught to teach; their methods, approaches, and activities are the same ones used when they were students. Some mentally retarded respond to these techniques and learn at a desirable rate. For other students such a rate is too fast and the dosage too large; for still others, the rate is too slow and portions too small. Instructors must have a thorough knowledge and understanding of sequences and progressions for water acclimation and swimming skills if they are to meet individual needs. Success and progress are more likely for the mentally retarded when skills are taught as a series of small coordinated steps—like building a brick wall where all bricks fit neatly together and one row emerges from the preceeding one.

Important in teaching the mentally retarded and implied by this discussion is the role of *repetition* in teaching swimming skills which also helps the student understand exactly what is expected of him and makes success more likely. *Much* reinforcement is needed so skills can be reduced to habit levels and can be performed with little or no conscious effort. The skills beginning swimmers must consciously think about become automatic with practice and repetition so that the experienced swimmer performs these same skills with little if any conscious effort. Many mentally retarded need to practice the same movements, skills, and strokes in a variety of ways under diverse conditions, and through many different approaches.

Instructors must be flexible and able to make adjustments in approaches, methods, and activities at a moment's notice according to the needs of the individual. Instructors must be alert to activities not challenging students and make necessary adjustments upward to regain their interest and motivation. Conversely, they must recognize signs indicating activities that are beyond the grasp and understanding of students and make these necessary adjustments. Programs based upon teaching the individual and meeting his specific needs require an instructor who knows the sequential progression of swimming skills, understands the mentally retarded, and is not afraid to deviate from the traditional and conventional.

Terminology

Swimming and the water provide activities and experiences in an environment which is completely new to many retardates—often words and concepts are new; old and familiar terms may be used in new ways and in an unfamiliar context. The swimming instructor must be certain he is communicating with the retarded in understandable ways and with familiar words. Words and speech patterns the retarded student brings with him to the swimming class, even though coll quial, questionable, and not gramatically correct, must be accepted and respected by the instructor. Accepting the student as he is can help establish rapport between instructor and student and provide a base for teaching him more acceptable and correct words and speech patterns. However, nothing can be taken for granted—often the simplest words and concepts must be explained and described in detail. A variety of visual aids—pictures, films, slides, the objects being described, and demonstration activities--can be effective in *showing* words and concepts, and in reinforcing other approaches.

Since many words and terms used in and around the swimming pool and in the instructional program may be new and unfamiliar to the retarded, instructors must be aware of them, explain them carefully when necessary, and use them in ways to avoid confusion and misunderstanding. Examples of words which may be in this category include--

up - down[2]	dress - undress	straight
over - under	roll over	bend
together - apart	breathe	reach
in - out	turn	jump
top - bottom	tuck	bathroom
right - left	recover	restroom
front - back	children	wash cloth
deep - shallow	swim	wash
push - pull	swimmer	various parts of the
float - sink	dive	body
boys - girls	ladder	various strokes
men - women	bottom line	appropriate words and
big - small	overflow	terms from other areas
fast - slow	gutter	of the student's expe-
loud - quiet	rail	rience which are appli-
open - close	shower	cable to the swimming
wet - dry	soap	program
deck - pool	towel	

Many swimming skills and aquatic activities can be introduced in the classroom, gymnasium, or on the pool deck where the retardate can learn the mechanics of a movement or skill, how to play a game, or the pattern of a relay. Familiar activities permit the instructor to place more emphasis upon water adjustment and acclimation when these activities are introduced in water. Everything should be done exactly the same in water as on land to assist the transition and transfer of these activities from land to water. Aquatic and swimming lead-up activities introduced on land should incorporate the same words and terms to be used in the water. This helps the retardate apply what he already knows in different situations and environments; he doesn't have to learn a new activity while becoming accustomed to water. The alert instructor can also use this approach to make tasks more challenging for the student--give him dual commands; have him make two or more adjustments to an activity learned on land; and make him attend to several tasks simultaneously.

---

[2]Often words and terms presented in pairs with opposite meanings help to clarify and reinforce their meanings with the retarded.

Transfer of Learning

Researchers in psychology and physical education, along with observant and understanding practitioners, have long realized that transfer in motor activity occurs only when muscles and muscle groups are used exactly in the same way. Lately, reports have indicated that a basic quality such as strength transfers only when muscles and muscle groups are used in the same movement and through the same range of motion. We have all been aware of the specificity of skills and movements of outstanding athletes who become specialized in only one aspect of a given sport.

Increasingly, learning--motor as well as cognitive--is being viewed as very specific; individuals attain levels of performance and skills not thought possible of them because of their lack of previous experience and an inadequate foundation. Why then do we need to concern ourselves with basic or foundation activities, low-organized activities, and specific lead-ups? Why shouldn't we concentrate on specific end results? Why shouldn't we focus only on specific strokes in teaching an individual to swim? Actually, what does transfer in aquatic programs?

Even if no transfer occurs, lower level activities and experiences are needed to give students--non-retarded as well as retarded, and those from enriched environments as well as the deprived--opportunities to achieve and succeed, to start and finish tasks, to take pride in what they do, and to build *concepts* which can be applied to other situations. This is also consistent with a true developmental approach, in which certain experiences are needed to ensure a sound progression from skill to skill and level to level.

Careful selection of activities, proper emphasis by instructors, and appropriate understanding of transfer itself are necessary if direct transfer is to occur from one activity to another. Certainly, concepts transfer--and can only be developed through participation in a wide variety of activities and experiences--and skills transfer when there are identical elements in movements. Instructors should carefully assess their reasons for including each activity, determine cause and effect relationships, and recognize that which transfers and that which is needed as a part of developmental progression as independent, though seemingly related, experience, which helps to prepare the participant for future levels of achievement. These factors are important considerations for all involved in instructional swimming programs.

Motivation

Recent reports and studies emphasize the importance of motivation if instructors are to reach the mentally retarded. There are those who feel progress and achievement in many motor activities and physical performance tasks are more indicative of participant interest and motivation than of motor or physical ability per se. These intangible and difficult to measure factors have been observed as especially affecting physical and motor performances of the mentally retarded. Success and fun contribute much to gaining interest and motivating the retarded in many different situations and activities.

There is no one way in which an instructor can be sure of reaching and motivating every student with whom he works. Methods and approaches successful for one instructor in a given situation with specific students will not necessarily be successful for the same instructor in another situation with different students. Another instructor may fail miserably if he uses methods and approaches someone else has found successful in another situation. Instructor-student interaction and the student's relationship with others in his group influence motivation. The activity itself, the community, and environmental factors are additional considerations which instructors must not overlook as affecting individual motivation.

Ideally students should participate because of inner desire and personal satisfactions derived. The retarded are not always motivated in this manner and additional techniques must often be introduced. Some retardates respond best to tangible rewards; some enter the water for candy received, stars placed on charts, or pictures taken.[3] The retarded student soon finds he can perform in such a way that inner satisfactions and good feelings develop. Gradually, sometimes dramatically fast, the retardate begins to participate because of the subtle effects of success which stimulate his desire to take part for intangible reasons. Initial external motivation has become internal.

Regardless of specific motivational methods and approaches, certain basic considerations are important—students experience success through participation in challenging, meaningful, and functional activities. This helps them out of their failure-frustration cycle as they develop better feelings about themselves and what they can do. Opportunities to perform for others—peers, instructors, parents, and guests help motivate students to participate, practice, progress, and provide additional ways for them to receive simple, but important, recognition of their achievements. Achievement and planned recognition need to go hand-in-hand throughout the program!

Instructor Expectation

Interest, motivation, challenge, and student achievement are all closely related to instructor expectation. If the swimming instructor guides the retarded into activities considerably above or below his level of ability and potential, little if any progress results, the student loses motivation, becomes disinterested, and does not develop desired skills. So often the instructor is influenced by preconceived ideas of what the retarded can and cannot do—he puts each in a little niche based on combinations of factors as I.Q., mental age, and chronological age, erroneously considering them absolute determinants of ability in all areas. This can affect the instructor's attitude toward and expectation of the retarded. When a retardate feels he is expected to fail, he

---

[3]Recent work with behavior modification techniques (operant conditioning) has given much encouragement to those who deal with the mentally retarded. Chapter VII of this publication deals with behavior modification techniques and how they can be applied to teaching the mentally retarded to swim.

is more likely to fail than in situations where he is expected to achieve and succeed. Instructor expectation affects the way in which the retardate conceives his role, the amount of success he experiences, and subtly affects the way in which the instructor deals with him. Recent studies have shown teacher expectation influences achievement of both retarded and non-retarded in the classroom. These same factors are present in the swimming class and can influence the retarded in learning to swim. The retarded are sensitive to these relationships; instructors must be equally alert and sensitive if they are to be effective and reach the retarded. *Emphasis must be upon the individual's ability not his disability; he should be encouraged, not discouraged; accentuate the positive not the negative.*

Evaluation[4]

Only through constant instructor evaluation can the swimming needs of a student be met. There are many specific instruments and ways to determine a student's progress in learning to swim. One of the best and most efficient ways to evaluate is to assess the student's ability to perform desired movements, skills, and strokes. The astute instructor observes the progress of students as a primary means of evaluation. As one skill is achieved the student is challenged with the next step in the progression. Instructors must know sequences of skills and movements so well they can make adjustments and deviate from usual and traditional progressions. *Evaluation is justified only as it contributes to instruction and is a part of the total instructional program.*

Awards

Tangible awards can provide additional incentive and motivation to mentally retarded in swimming programs. So many retardates have had so little opportunity to participate and experience success in swimming programs that few have ever won any kind of an award--for them even simple awards have great significance. A number of organizations--Red Cross, Y.M.C.A., Canadian Association for Retarded Children--have progressive swimming award programs; other agencies have less elaborate but equally defined programs by which students are rewarded for performing specific skills or reaching certain levels of achievement. Some of the most effective systems and programs have been developed by individuals for local use. Many different award systems have been successful with the mentally retarded--

1. *Ribbons* of various colors have an *official* look when cut with pinking shears; stars and other insignia pasted on them reflect additional progress and subsequent awards.

2. *Cards* or *progress sheets* indicate specific levels of achievement; interest is added for the retardate by giving each level

---

[4] See pages 31-36 for illustrative examples of evaluation forms which have been used successfully.

Tadpole

AWARDS

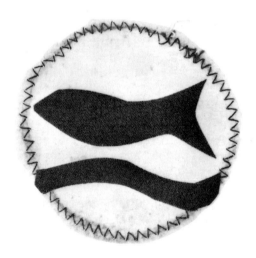

Fish

Dolphin

Award Crests used in swimming programs in Charleston, West Virginia.

These crests are made by retarded adolescents and young adults in Faith Workshop -- they not only give those who receive them a sense of accomplishment, but help those who make them feel that they too are making a contribution to the program.

a clever name--*landlubber, wader, dunker, diver, mermaid, aquaman, surfer, beachcomber, frogman,* etc. Different kinds of ships, fish, or other items of interest to the retarded can be used to designate various classes or categories.

3. *Badge systems* similar to those used by the Red Cross or Y.M.C.A. can be developed locally.

4. *Swimming Honor Rolls* display the names of all students who master certain skills or attain specific levels of achievement. Determine skills and levels of achievement according to the ability of those taking part in the program. Several levels of achievement are needed for each skill or stroke so all students will have an opportunity to make the honor roll and be challenged to improve performances to attain increasingly difficult categories.

5. *Halls of Fame* display pictures of all students who have particularly outstanding achievements--the individual with the fastest time in the 25-yard swim for each age level; the individual who bobs the most; the one who walks across the pool the fastest. Determine these categories according to the level and ability of those taking part in the program.

Appropriate ceremonies, no matter how simple, add much to the impact of awards and are great sources of enjoyment for students. These ceremonies can be a part of regularly scheduled programs--assemblies, council rings, all group gatherings--or especially scheduled--parent nights, visitor days, and awards assemblies.

Discipline

Safety in and around water demands well-disciplined individuals and classes. Attention to detail, good organization, anticipation of problems, and consistency in dealing with the retarded are essential to good discipline. Many retardates feel secure in activities and programs where procedures are well established and what is expected of them is made clear in terms they understand. Some retardates are unaccustomed to personal freedom, program flexibility, and instructor permissiveness. They are unable to handle these situations because they have not had opportunities and experiences to develop an appropriate foundation. These are important considerations in swimming programs for the mentally retarded because of dangers inherent to pools, lakes, and similar swimming sites. Some activities within the swimming program itself can promote emotional control and self-discipline; instructors should consciously capitalize upon such activities. Sound discipline is built upon a positive approach; threats, corporal measures, or intimidation are no more effective with the mentally retarded than with the non-retarded--deal with each student as if he is six feet five inches tall and 250 pounds! The retarded learn what is expected of them and how to react and respond under a variety of conditions from instructors who are consistent in handling situations and individuals. Instructors must develop disciplinary techniques and approaches appropriate for each situation. In some instances withholding swimming privileges for a short time or even a class period may be an effective disciplinary measure--but only for misbehavior in activities related to the swimming program. When disciplinary situations arise, instructors need to assess the situation and determine *why* the undesirable behavior occurred. A productive teaching-learning situation demands good discipline; good discipline is promoted by a teaching-learning situation which holds the interest and attention of the student.

Swimming Readiness

Instructors teaching the mentally retarded to swim should have broad knowledge of physical growth and motor development and be skilled and competent in a variety of swimming activities for pre-swimmers, beginning swimmers, and for students in more advanced categories. A variety of activities conducted in the home, classroom, and gymnasium should be a part of the complete instructional swim program.

In the home the child learns water is a necessity; it is his friend and helpmate for health and cleanliness. When left in bath tubs, wading pools, or troughs, water can spell tragedy and catastrophy. Appreciation and respect for water are first taught in the home; those who enjoy water and have no history of frightening experiences usually adjust readily to the instructional swim program.

Swimming readiness can be developed in many ways in the classroom. Stories about fun in the water, pictures, flip charts, and scrapbooks about pools, discussions about swimming pool dress and behavior, information about locker and shower rooms, and data about and explanation of swim strokes can be effectively used in the swimming readiness program. These topics can become lively subject matter for reading readiness sessions, word association activities, story telling, and dramatic play; simple addition and subtraction can be incorporated through a problem solving approach. Movies such as *Teaching Johnny to Swim* (American Red Cross) and *I'm No Fool in Water* (Walt Disney Production), filmstrips, slides, single concept loop films, and other audiovisual materials can be helpful to the student and instructor. Basins of water can be used for demonstration and training--feel the water, blow on the water, put your face in the water, put your face in the water and blow, open your eyes when your face is under water are a few of the directions and problems an instructor can give his students.

Similarly, the gymnasium provides another environment in which students can be prepared for swimming before actually going to the pool or lake. Activities that increase motor and perceptual development should be included in the pre-swim program. Locomotor activities like crawling, creeping, running, jumping, hopping, skipping, galloping, and leaping; balancing activities on beams and boards; tumbling and gymnastic activities on mats, trampoline, horizontal bar, parallel bars, and side horse are all valuable and contribute to

51

development of motor ability and physical skills basic to success in swimming. Generally, the sounder the base of motor development and physical fitness, the more likely an individual is to succeed in a variety of activities, including swimming. Similarly, swimming can be a stimulus and an activity to promote improved physical fitness and motor ability. Swimming is also a subject area around which many important educational experiences and opportunities--mental, emotional, and social, as well as physical--can be developed.

Orientation

When a student is first brought to the pool site much instruction and orientation are usually still needed before he actually goes into the water. Much of the preparation for this stage should be done in the classroom, at home, and in similar non-pool situations. Parents, teachers, and others who deal with the student can contribute to initial orientation and prepare him for the first pool session. They influence early attitudes toward water, swimming, instruction, and are in important positions to supplement the direct efforts of the swimming instructional staff throughout the program. Prior to the first pool session the student may be taken on a tour of locker and shower rooms. He needs to know where the toilet facilities are located, be instructed in their proper use, and taught to operate the showers. Proper use of lockers, locker room rules and regulations, and general health and safety practices need to be discussed. Location of first aid equipment and facial tissues should be included in the initial stages of pool orientation. *Nothing can be left to chance.* Even routine pool procedures such as the use of bathing caps for girls and procedures to follow in leaving the pool to go to the rest room must be spelled out in clear, concise, and understandable language. Instructors and aides should learn to care for special needs of participants from the time they enter the locker room. Some students will need assistance dressing and undressing. Wheelchairs, braces, and prosthetic devices need to be handled with know-how, ease, and confidence. Many aides and assistants will need such instruction prior to the first class session. Many of these responsibilities can be assigned to assistants and aides so instructors will have more time to plan the instructional program, give individual attention, evaluate participants, and work right in the pool. With more capable students check-in, check-out, or buddy systems may be considered to free instructors from locker room routines and give them even more time for their major concern--instruction. An interesting and happy experience in the locker room sets the stage for security and safety in the pool.

After taking a good soap shower and dressing in swim suits, students are taken to the pool area and finally enter the water.

The retardate needs to become familiar with the pool area itself. He needs the opportunity to walk around the pool and to talk about its different features--the water is your friend, it is warm and pleasant; the pool has shallow and deep water--for many retardates concepts of shallow and deep will be completely new; we have loads of fun in the water; this part of the pool is for beginners and that for advanced swimmers; this is the diving board, and this the diving area.

All aides involved in the program may need to assist in preparing and bringing students to the pool. Often swimming programs for the multiply handicapped-mentally retarded require a considerably larger staff than programs in which participants have only intellectual or mental deficits. These classes may require one-to-one instructor-student ratios to teach effectively the most elementary skills. Instructors should be alert to recognize individuals who need more interaction with their peers than is possible in a one-to-one situation. All students should be given opportunities to become more socially aware and to develop social skills in groups with gradually increasing numbers. For example, an instructor or aide and his student who have been in a one-to-one situation may join another instructor or aide with his student who have been in this same type situation to form a group of four. Within the larger group each student has the security of his own instructor. One instructor then withdraws leaving his student in a new social situation; when the first instructor returns, the other withdraws. Reaction and responses of the students are noted to determine their readiness for expanding group activity and greater social interaction. As students show need, interest, and readiness to expand their social contacts, this same procedure can be used to enlarge groups. This approach has been particularly effective with timid, withdrawn, and lower level retardates as a means of gradually acclimating them to and involving them in group activity.

Each participant must be looked upon and accepted as an individual of worth and dignity who can and should be helped. Mentally retarded have the same basic needs, drives, and problems as other students of a comparable chronological age. Acceptance, understanding, and tender loving care (TLC) are of utmost importance in establishing rapport and in developing a good relationship between student and instructor.

The instructor should develop a sequential plan to meet individual needs and to make progress and achievement possible for each student even in the most elementary of movements, skills, and activities. Special needs, unique problems, and specific knowledge about each swimmer must be considered if the swimming program is to be individualized. *Routine, repetition,* and *relaxation* are important and should be a part of each lesson. The retarded feel secure with a regular routine; they feel comfortable when patterns are consistent with procedures and schedules with which they are completely familiar. Since many retardates learn in slow motion, movements and skills, as well as concepts often must be presented in a variety of ways so the student can have many different opportunities in which to execute and practice them. Too often instructors forget that the ability to relax is a prerequisite for good coordination. Emphasis and practice must be provided so the student can develop the ability to relax in water while executing and coordinating desired movements, skills, and strokes. Good coordination promotes relaxation; helping the individual learn to relax in turn helps him develop, execute, and coordinate strokes. The swimming instructor can leave none of this to chance; every necessary element must be planned for and structured into each lesson. Interest and motivation are prime requisites to gain and hold a student's attention. To help accomplish this some form of recognition should be given to reinforce the swimmer's efforts every time he executes a skill or activity

53

properly. A pat on the back, an arm around the shoulders, words of praise, and congratulations, a well-timed handshake, or a sincere smile are all quite effective with the mentally retarded for these purposes.

Verbal and non-verbal techniques are essential if the instructor is to reach everyone taking part in the swimming program. Words used must be understood by the participant. Oral expression, even though slang and not grammatically correct, provides an avenue of understanding for the retardate. Effective communication between the student and his instructor is absolutely necessary if progress and growth are to occur. New words may be introduced as a part of each lesson to broaden the student's vocabulary and help him replace less desirable words he has been using. Other means of communication must be used with students who have visual handicaps, impaired hearing, and those who require different kinds of sensory stimulation. Explicit verbalization, tactile approaches, and kinesthetic techniques where body parts are moved through desired movements are important techniques with the blind. Demonstrations, pictures, films, slides, signs telling what to do, other visual procedures, and talking distinctly and directly to the participant so he may lip read are methods used with hearing impaired. Instructors and aides who teach the mentally retarded must be constantly alert for ways to make activities and approaches more effective. Improvise, innovate, and use many different techniques to teach the simplest water adjustment activities and the most advanced swimming skills.

Entering the Water

Many methods and approaches are available to assist the instructor and to encourage the student to enter the water. No set pattern or pat procedure will guarantee success with all students; *each student must be approached as an individual.* The interaction between student and instructor is an important factor in building the necessary foundation; an instructor who has rapport with a student often can reach and do things with him when another instructor can do nothing with the same individual. Every aspect of the instructional program and the environment in which it is conducted must be considered to make success more likely for *every* student. In no other part of the program are these factors more important than when introducing the student to the water for the first time.

Pool entry and water adjustment can be approached simultaneously. A student sits on the side of the pool and dangles his feet in the water. He can splash himself gently, feel the water on various parts of his body, and develop a feeling of comfort and ease around water. Water only a few inches deep may be necessary during this crucial time if the timid and fearful are to progress. Portable plastic wading pools placed on the pool deck should not be overlooked as devices to aid these students at this stage of the program.

The student can sit on the side of the pool or stand in shallow water and use a wash cloth,[5] a familiar item, to learn how water feels on various

_____

[5] See page 56 for suggested activities with a wash cloth.

parts of his body. At no point in teaching swimming **is** it more important for the student to have fun and for the instructor to *make haste slowly* than during these initial stages in the water. Each individual has his own timetable for progress which must be respected by the instructor; a predetermined sequence and rate cannot be superimposed upon each individual. Contrary to this approach, the instructor must *challenge each student and encourage him as an individual* to try new activities and to develop new skills. As the individual begins to feel relaxed and confident around and in the water have him move through it -- walk, run, jump, hop, skip, gallop, and leap. These, other basic movements, and mimetic activities are excellent to help the student get accustomed to water and how it affects him. Activities at this level may be performed with or without instructor aid or other kinds of assistance. The student's ability to work independently will promote a feeling of *being at home in the water*. Many games, relays, and low organized activities[6] can be used to promote adjustment and acclimation to the water. As the individual gains in confidence he should move to water of increasing depths; conversely, deeper water can promote greater confidence on the part of the individual.

Adaptations and Innovations

Activities from home, classroom, and gymnasium are easily adapted for use in the water. These are activities with which the student is familiar; he already knows them so the new element is the transfer to water. In this way, instruction moves from the known to the unknown, the simple to the complex, and the concrete to the abstract. Many mentally retarded respond to instruction at this level when their arms and legs are moved through desired motions and movements to supplement and reinforce verbal and visual stimuli. The multiply handicapped, the very poorly coordinated, retardates functioning at lower levels, the visually handicapped, and those with hearing impairments especially need this type of instruction. As the student gets the feel of what is expected of him he proceeds more rapidly, develops confidence in himself, and has a feeling of comfort and ease around water that is necessary before instruction in specific skills and strokes can be introduced successfully.

Some students must have individual assistance and attention to help them overcome their fear of water. At first the instructor may have to hold the small child, walk around in shallow water with him, put water on him gently, immerse his arms and legs, bounce up and down with him, and generally have fun. Instructors and aides should talk with students to discover their interests, to help establish rapport, and to gain their confidence. This all helps the student feel more at home in the pool environment. The instructor should *never* break his word to his student--if a student is told he will not get water in his eyes or have his head go under water, it is of utmost importance that these things do not happen. One accidental slip of this kind can undo hours, days, and even weeks of effort that will be most difficult to counteract. As in

----

[6]See Chapter V for specific activities of this nature.

55

other areas of work with the retarded, adjustment to water may be a rather rapid process or it may take several visits to the pool in which a variety of approaches is used; it all depends upon the individual and his instructor.

Existing methods and materials used in teaching the mentally retarded to swim need to be reviewed, evaluated, and reclassified. Many swimming instructors feel the basic methods of teaching swimming need to be upgraded. The instructor must think, analyze, and plan according to each individual's function and needs. The creative instructor will appeal to the individual retardate with whom he is working by finding appropriate devices and introducing new methods and approaches. The swimming instructor must be a psychologist, educator, friend, benefactor, and analyst combined!

Assistive Devices

Methods which capitalize upon familiarity and security have proved effective with the mentally retarded. Since most children have from early infancy had their faces washed with soft damp cloths, this *old friend* is brought to class. There is no fear since water is not thrown into the child's eyes and there is no splashing; the child progresses at his own rate and has fun while he learns.

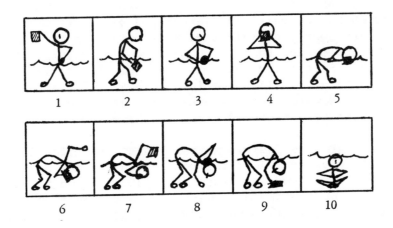

Many children are too short to touch the bottom in the shallow end of the pool; a towel held by two people brings the bottom of the pool up to the child! There are many ways in which a towel can be used to aid the timid child in getting accustomed to water--float on it, change positions, move through the water, move along it, move the arms, kick the feet and legs. During this time the instructor must be alert for natural movements

56

as clues to strokes and skills to teach the individual even though they don't follow any particular pattern or sequence.

Have the child *balance* on a plank--12 foot 2 X 4, 2 X 6, 2 X 8, or 2 X 10-- lie down, roll over, and move along it. As he gains confidence encourage him to stay on the plank and to use natural arm and leg movements.

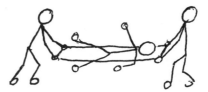

A length of rope can be used in the same way as a towel or plank. As the child gains ability and confidence, lower one end of the support so he actually keeps parts of his body afloat himself. Gradually lower the entire device so the child floats completely on his own. Keep the device close to the student in the early stages so support can be reapplied if he should start to sink. Even non-swimmers can hold one end of a towel, plank or rope--these simple devices can work wonders for an instructor!

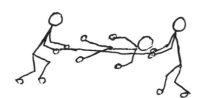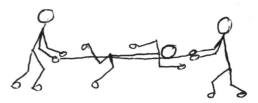

Other easily obtained items can be used to help support the beginning swimmer and assist him as he moves through the water. Assistive devices should supplement other instructional methods and approaches and *must never be allowed to become a crutch upon which the student depends--they should be used as assistive devices and teaching aids only.* Seldom if ever should a student be allowed to use an assistive device for an entire period. In addition, it is recommended that assistive devices be used only in shallow water. Among the advantages and purposes for assistive devices are:

1.   To support a body part as an aid in developing a skill or
     part of a stroke in which other body parts are used. Ex-
     ample: use a kick board to support the upper torso while
     practicing a kick or to support the legs while practicing
     arm movements.

2. To provide experiences for the beginning swimmer to get the *feel* of a movement through kinesthetic feedback as the muscles send messages back to the brain so body parts can be located and their movements known even though the parts are out of the field of vision. Examples: use instructor support or appropriate flotation devices to get the feel of the back float; use appropriate flotation devices to make propulsion through the water possible so that the student gets the feel of a stroke.

3. To provide specially needed support for students with specific handicaps--amputees, hemiplegics, paraplegics. Example: use flippers on arm or leg stubs of amputees to aid propulsion through water.

4. To provide experiences for the student to move through the water and get the idea and feel of locomotion. Example: use an approved life jacket or vest with a beginning swimmer so he can safely and successfully move through the water-- he not only gets the feel of locomotion in water but has fun as he gains confidence and learns to feel at home in water; he can also take part in other activities with his peers and talk about how he *swims*!

5. To serve as a counter-balance to minimize or eliminate unnecessary and unwanted movements and overflow actions. Example: use wrist or ankle weights to make undesirable movements more difficult in the affected arm or leg so as to smooth out the stroke and make it a more coordinated whole.

6. To help the student develop confidence so he will feel more relaxed and comfortable in the water and be more receptive to instruction and teaching.

7. To help the student develop a feeling of buoyancy and the ability to let the water support him.

Many assistive techniques[7] can be of value to the instructor in different stages of teaching the mentally retarded to swim:

----

[7]While some instructors prefer to use inner tubes of various sizes to help students develop certain swimming skills and movements, many questions have been raised about their safety. For example, special attention must be given to protect students from injury by the valve stem of the inner tube. Valve stems may be taped securely to the side of the tube, covered with a tennis ball, or removed and replaced by a screw which fits flush with the tube. The use of inner tubes should be confined to shallow water and with students who possess sufficient skill and ability to handle themselves in the event that they are dumped into the water unexpectedly. In no instance should inner tubes be permitted without direct supervision of those using them.

1. Have students bracket against the side of the pool to work
    on various elements of strokes--kick while on the stomach,
    kick while on the back, move arms while the feet are secured
    in the overflow.

2. Use another person to support certain body parts while desired
    movements are executed with other body parts--as buoyancy and
    confidence develop, less support is necessary.

3. Use kickboards, oars, paddle boards, or surf boards, to sup-
    port the legs, arms, or middle portion of the body according
    to the need and ability of the student.

4. Use broom sticks with plastic bleach bottles or other ob-
    jects attached (bar bell fashion) as floats.

5. Use plastic bleach or detergent bottles as floats; gradually
    increase the amount of water in the bottles to reduce the
    buoyant effect upon the body.

6. Use manufactured aquatic bar bells much in the same manner
    as the devices described in 3, 4, and 5 above.

7. Use styrofoam such as that used for flotation docks and
    other devices to provide support for parts of the body
    as needed; reduce support as the student progresses to
    provide only the amount of assistance needed.

8. Use water wings, life jackets, and similar flotation
    devices to assist individuals with specific problems and
    difficulties.

Human support can be used effectively in many ways--hold hands with the
student and walk with him in shallow water; have the student take a few steps
to reach your hands; support the student in various positions, gradually re-
leasing him but always reassuring him that your hands are still close by if
support is needed.

Swimming skills and movements can be developed and activities practiced
out of and away from water. Virtually all of these approaches capitalize
upon kinesthetic feedback where the student gets the feel of the proper mechanics of the skill or movement. When the student goes into the water he may experience some minor difficulties in executing the movements or skills performed
with devices out of and away from the water because of the pressure and resistance offered by the water. Generally, these problems and inefficiencies
are short lived as the student quickly applies what he has learned with these
special devices and approaches. Among the innumerable possibilities are:

1. Do activities on mats, the floor, across a chair or bed in
    such a way that the arms and/or legs are used in a variety

of movements simulating swimming skills or strokes.

2. Use scooter boards for activities so students can perform movements to promote development of specific swimming movements, skills, or strokes.

3. Make swimming trainers or platforms so the student can simulate swimming movements and develop additional strength through an application of overload procedures.

4. Attach ropes in such a way that the student may pull himself across the pool while holding the ropes, walk between them, or use them for support while kicking or practicing arm strokes.

An important element in all teaching approaches is *fun--keep the fun in fundamentals!* This is important to consider in the teaching of breath control. Some ways to introduce blowing, holding, and controlling the breath have been suggested in the section dealing with uses of the wash cloth.[8] Other ways in which an instructor can help a reluctant child develop and practice this most important skill include--blow through straws or pipes, blow water out of the palm or off the back of the hand, blow a variety of objects which float such as ping-pong balls, plastic baby food jars, or colored corks. As the student improves, the object can be changed to make blowing more difficult and challenging--bigger and heavier objects are more difficult to move by blowing since they require more effort and breath control. These activities can also be used to teach concepts such as color and number identification. A variety of breathing activities help the student develop greater functional lung capacity and more effective respiration.

Often an individual who will not go under water on his own will do so without thinking when his attention is upon another task. Many times children who have been afraid of water go under with no hesitation while using a wash cloth; the same is true when they are asked to duck for objects or to bring them up from the bottom of the pool. Objects which can be **used** for retrieving include weighted *plastic* baby food jars or tops, weighted *plastic* toys, rubber balls or pucks, rubber rings, and weights. Perceptual, arithmetic, letter and word identification, spelling, and other concepts and skills can be reinforced and taught through these activities. The overall possibilities are limited only by the instructor's imagination and ingenuity.

---

[8] See page 56.

Land drills -- capitalizing on kinesthetic feedback to get the feel of the mechanics of an arm stroke. DeKalb County Schools, DeKalb, Georgia.

Double support -- learning to kick while holding a rail and getting support from the instructor. Recreation Services for the Handicapped, Memphis, Tennessee.

"Look mom, no hands." Some need support even in shallow water.

Security and confidence -- instructor assists a beginner on his back. Longview YMCA, Longview, Washington - Jan Fardell Photos

61

Progress -- instructor acting as support in the prone position for TMR student. Longview YMCA, Longview, Washington. Jan Fardell Photos

And away we go -- youngsters hold and climb on kickboards. Longview YMCA, Longview, Washington. Jan Fardell Photos

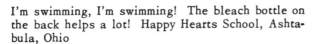

I'm swimming, I'm swimming! The bleach bottle on the back helps a lot! Happy Hearts School, Ashtabula, Ohio

It doesn't hurt to help! *Water wings* and an understanding instructor help. Recreation Services for the Handicapped, Memphis, Tennessee

62

Two pieces of foam flutterboard laced together with clothesline -- this floatboard lets Kenny swim. Board should be secured firmly with a square knot, usually at waist level. These devices are very successfully used with normal and handicapped children at the YWCA Pool in St. Joseph, Michigan.

"Kick and blow bubbles! Oh, very good!" One professional swimming instructor and a corps of volunteers work with Kenny and his classmates once a week for one-half hour during school time. He attends Gard School for trainable retarded children, a part of the public school system of St. Joseph, Michigan.

"Pull and pull and pull . . ." Kenny sits on teacher's knee as she helps him move his arms in a freestyle-type stroke. Kenny has cerebral palsy involving right arm and leg.

"I'll hold you tight! Stretch out your arms and pull and pull!" With one hand on his tummy and one on his back the teacher gives support until Kenny can make arms and legs all go at the same time.

On his own! Though his stroke may not be exactly perfect, his joy and sense of accomplishment are. Kenny has had about 15 hours of pool time. He jumps in from a standing position, and can swim several lengths of the pool. Some of the less handicapped boys are beginning to be able to swim without their floatboards.

"Make your toes come out--lay your head on my shoulder . . ." Teacher attempts to move Kenny's arms in elementary backstroke. He is not happy on his back, though some of his classmates do very well this way. Support is needed for the head in most cases as they tend to arch and duck themselves.

Photos by Lois Rea.

A simple way to determine whether or not a student is breathing effectively with his head in the water is to place your hands on his face near the back of his cheek. If he is breathing correctly, air going in and out of the mouth can easily be felt. *Arthur Peter Bieri, Instructor for the Mentally Retarded and Handicapped Swimming, Stillwater, Oklahoma.*

While there is difference of opinion regarding the role of low organized games, relays, and other similar *play activities* as a part of instructional swimming programs, they can be valuable and contribute *when used for a purpose and to achieve specific objectives.*[9] Select play activities with which the student is familiar so the only new element is the environment in which he finds himself. This not only provides a familiar activity but presents a situation in which the student's attention is focused on something other than the water. He gets completely engrossed in the activity, forgets about

_____

[9]See Chapter V for a detailed list of games, relays, and low organized activities applicable to and appropriate for all levels of instructional swimming programs involving the mentally retarded.

the water, and often does things not attempted previously.[10]

Those who work with the mentally retarded find music and rhythmical activities very effective. Soft or lively background music can be effective in promoting a desired mood or attitude; it can connote fun and lead to pleasurable experiences for the student. Appropriate music may motivate and stimulate the passive, soothe the hyperactive, and promote a level of participation and performance not attained without it.

Movement Exploration[11]

Movement exploration is a planned series of problem-solving experiences through which a child learns to understand, control, and improve the many ways his body moves. This method of teaching movement has grown out of educational gymnastics in English schools.

In using movement exploration as a teaching method, the instructor attempts to help the child learn *what his body can do, where his body can move,* and *how it can move.* Children have *readiness* for reading and other cognitive skills--the same is true of movement readiness. Each child comes to us with his individual backlog of experience; his movement skills and movement potentials are products of that experience. The instructor's task is to help the child find new experiences that will have meaning for him.

Physical education has recently been placing great stress on the development of physical fitness. Physical fitness can be improved rapidly with a suitable developmental program but the results are transient unless physical activity is continued. Those who believe that it is important for the child to learn about basic movement also believe that such learning might make a long-lasting contribution to fitness because it focuses upon helping the child know the joy and benefit of the use of his body.

Often we have taught physical education to the hypothetical average student--we have taught as if all children learn in the same way. The *show and tell* methods of teaching--the teacher shows, the pupil copies--often used to teach sports skills may impose movement which is meaningless. A movement discovered by a child for himself, because he can *do* the movement, is within his reach of capability and can have exciting results. Movement education provides an atmosphere for real thinking in the gymnasium, on the

---

[10]Organized water play is a part of the complete swimming program and is a medium particularly suited to the early stages of instruction when water acclimation and adjustment are emphasized.

[11]This section on *Movement Exploration* was prepared by Elizabeth C. Umstead, Associate Professor of Physical Education, University of North Carolina--Greensboro.

play field, or in the swimming pool. Motivation to think and to solve problems results in richer experiences and a deeper understanding of the body in movement.

Perhaps the greatest advantage for this method of teaching comes from the independence it provides each child. He learns to invent, to find his own way to move according to his experience level, and to realize the capacities of his body. Because there is no norm against which he passes or fails, he learns not to be afraid of being different, he loses his self-consciousness, and begins to enjoy expressive movement. It gives the child an opportunity to direct himself and to rely upon himself to find answers that are neither more nor less then he is able to give. Thus, through exploration of what his body can do, the child enhances his self-identification and his self-understanding. He begins to know what he is, what his body is, and what his body can do.

Movement Exploration for the Mentally Retarded Student

The method of teaching movement by the exploration or problem-solving approach has many implications for teaching the mentally retarded. Many activities are conducted on a one-to-one basis, or where one instructor has a small number of students so the exploration approach can be conducted under the most favorable circumstances and its advantages often recognized more readily. This method of teaching seems particularly well-suited to meet the specific needs of mentally retarded children. More important, within this method is an inherent design which emphasizes progress for the individual while keeping foremost in mind his needs, abilities, and limitations. The method might be examined in light of some of the stated needs of mentally retarded students.

1. *A need for better control of his body*
   Movement exploration attempts to get at the core of movement so the individual might learn what his body can do and how he, as one individual with the total potential at his command—his experience, his skills, and limitations—might master movement skills best.

2. *A need for vigorous activity*
   Obesity is common to many mentally retarded children because of lack of sufficient vigorous activity. Movement exploration affords a method which assures that children are active most of the time, and are not waiting to take turns, listening to long explanations by the instructor, or watching others perform. Each child is occupied all of the time, solving problems in his own way and moving at his own speed.

3. *A need for self-expression*
   Self-expression is implicit in movement exploration for it is highly individualized except when problems are specifically designed for group cooperation.

4. *A need for confidence*
   Competition to *do a skill correctly* or to meet a pre-estab-
   lished norm is often stifling; great confidence can come
   from solving a movement problem which demands no more than
   an expression of self.

5. *A need for the joy of achievement*
   Success can come from mastering a physical problem, such as
   responding in an individualized way to a movement problem
   which requires no more than that the individual respond within the limits of his ability. This may be the first taste
   of success for some mentally retarded students.

Movement Exploration and Teaching Swimming to the Mentally Retarded

The exploration method is useful and effective in teaching all types
of movement skills--swimming is no exception. Many swimming instructors
have used this method at some time, especially when teaching elementary
water-adjustment activities to young or beginning students. Water-play and
simple game-like situations are often organized to allow the student to
explore his new environment on first entering the water. To teach swimming
by an exploratory method requires that all skills planned for a class be
organized as problem-solving situations and presented so the individual student has freedom to explore and solve problems in a way that is unique to
his own abilities.

The implications in this method for teaching swimming to mentally retarded students seem patently clear and almost demanding. Since mentally
retarded students often have other handicaps which make adjustments in teaching method mandatory, it seems advantageous to adopt a method which has a
built-in concern for individual differences.

In teaching swimming, as in other movement skills, the instructor and
student are concerned with certain basic elements of movement. Swimming
differs only in that the student experiences movement in a totally new
environment. Because water can support the body, the student is confronted
with a new concept not experienced fully before--this concept is buoyancy.
Aspects of basic movement with which he is familiar must now be related to
the new environment but many movement fundamentals, if mastered in other
skill areas, can be readily transferred and coordinated with the new element
of buoyancy.

Movement problems in swimming may be built around these basic considerations:

Awareness of self in the water - adjustment and much time spent
on feeling at home in the water.

Awareness of possibilities for movement of the body - exploration of *what* the body can do.

Awareness of qualities of movement in water - exploration of time, force and space. This awareness would be concerned with *how* the body moves in water--balance, rhythm, speed, body positions and relationships of body parts, space concepts and breath control.

Following are some brief *examples* of problems the instructor may use to motivate students to explore movements involved in swimming skills. Movement problems are always designed for a specific situation and a specific student; these are merely representative samples of types of problems that might be set for a mentally retarded student first learning to swim.

Breath Control

Can you breathe by just letting air go in your mouth and come out your mouth?
Can you pretend to blow bubbles in the air?
Can you catch some water and hold it in both hands?
Can you blow bubbles in the water in your hands?
Can you blow bubbles by putting your mouth down in the water?
Who can get wet all over?
Who can stoop down and get wet all over and blow bubbles while under the water?
Can you stoop down and get wet all over, and stay down while I count to five?
Can you count to five while under the water?
Can you touch your toes with one hand?
Can you touch a foot with each hand?

Body Awareness

Can you stand on one foot in the water?
Can you balance in shallow water on one hand and one foot? on two hands?
Can you get one foot higher than your head while keeping your hands on the bottom of the pool? two feet?
Can you sit on the bottom of the pool?
Can you make your buttlocks (seat, rump) go higher than your head?
Can you hold on to the edge of the pool and lie flat on the water on your back? on your face?
Can you hold on, lie flat on your face, then curl your whole body and stand up?
Can you curl, then stretch out?
Can you stoop down and put your elbow on the bottom of the pool?
Can you kneel on the bottom of the pool on one knee? on two knees?
Can you hold your partner's (or instructor's) two hands and the two of you jump up and down together?
Can you sit on the bottom of the pool together still holding hands?

Can you pick up coins (stones, etc.) from the bottom of the
pool?

Space and Body Awareness - (Stretch a rope across an area in shallow water.)

Can you step over the rope?
Can you jump over the rope with two feet?
Can you go over hands first?
Can you go under the rope?
Can you go under feet first? hands first? head first?
Can you go over the rope sideways? backwards?
Can you go under the rope any other ways? sideways?
    backwards?
Can you hold the kickboard in front of you, stretch out and
    go over the rope? faster this time?
How did you make the board and your body go faster? Can you
    do it with the body in another position?

Locomotion

Can you touch two pool walls and come back quickly to your
    space?
Can you move through the water in any other direction?
Which way is fastest? Why?
Try moving fast and slow through the water. What helps you
    move?
Can you run through the water using your hands to help you
    move?
What other ways can the hands help? Try other ways.

Locomotion with Flotation Device - (Use kickboards, or other flotation devices.)

Can you hold onto the board and stretch out your body in the
    water? Then curl and stand up?
Can you hold the board, stretch out and make the board go for-
    ward as you hold it?
What did you use? Can you go faster?
Can you do the same thing with your face in the water?
Can you make the board turn to one side and change direction?
    How did you do this?

Circuit and Interval Training

Circuit and interval training can be adapted to the swimming pool and
used in the instructional program to help develop specific skills and movements and to improve elements of physical fitness which contribute to the
student's overall success in the water. Circuit training is based upon an
approach in which students move among different stations at their own rate
according to their levels of fitness and skill. Interval training is based

upon an approach in which students perform a series of activities at their own levels or paces for a specified length of time. In each system everyone is active with no time wasted. Since pool time is generally limited, circuit and interval training provide an opportunity for maximum student participation. Circuit and interval training can be used at the beginning or end of a period before or after breaking into specific instructional groups; these are group activities in which swimmers of greatly varying abilities can take part together. Stations can be used to develop general or specific skills and movements. Establish stations so students can move from one to another after doing a given number of repetitions in an activity--ten flutter kicks, twelve crawl movements of the arms, fifteen rhythmic breaths, two objects brought up from the bottom. Activities at each station can be adapted and adjusted according to the class and the students. As a student gains in proficiency and confidence the tasks asked of him at each station are made increasingly difficult and challenging. Charts, motivational devices, and other modifications of more formal and highly structured circuits can be adapted and used with retardates of different abilities and functional levels. The student's reading level is not in itself a limiting factor in circuit training.[12]

There are several variables in an interval approach--time of execution, number of repetitions in a given time interval, rest interval between sets, and number of sets. By changing any one of the variables a greater challenge may be provided. An illustrative series might include--bob one minute, bracket and flutter kick one minute, kick from the back one minute, and tread water one minute. Any stroke or skill may be broken down into its component parts for interval training as unrelated activities can be used in a series. Interesting variations can be incorporated within the interval approach--have students do as many repetitions as they can in a given time period or time how long it takes them to do a predetermined number of repetitions. Interval training permits the instructor to focus upon skills or fitness by changing the emphasis. In order to achieve maximum benefit from interval training, a student must have minimum levels of strength, endurance, agility, flexibility, coordination, and balance.

Some instructors have found a combination circuit-interval approach effective with the mentally retarded. Students remain at each station for a specified length of time--ten seconds, thirty seconds, one minute. In this way everyone moves from station-to-station at the same time which reduces confusion, eliminates waiting in line at certain stations, and minimizes unnecessary movement. As students improve in ability and fitness, the time spent at each station can be gradually increased. When practical, instructors or aides should be at each station to provide greater individual attention for each student.

------

[12]See *Challenge* (AAHPER, Washington, D. C.) Vol. II, Nos. 1, 2, 3, (Sept. 1966, Nov. 1966, and Jan. 1967) for information about circuit training adapted for the mentally retarded.

After the student develops certain basic swimming skills and movements he may be taught more advanced activities. At this level slight modification of traditional and conventional approaches may be used successfully. The complete aquatic program for the mentally retarded should include games of higher organization (e.g., water polo, basketball, and volleyball), life saving techniques (e.g., elementary assists as well as personal safety), boating including canoeing and sailing, competitive swimming and diving, and synchronized swimming. Given opportunity and provided a progressive, meaningful, and sequential program, the retarded can develop levels of swimming proficiency and skill which will amaze even the most optimistic--*keys to such success are meaningful instruction, significant activities, and an early start.*

Success, as demonstrated by a simple dive, for a mentally retarded child. *Jan Fardell Photo.*

TEACHING PROGRESSIONS

Learning to feel safe, free, and comfortable in the water. The first step--and it is fun! *Longview YMCA, Longview, Washington*

Classes in which the mentally retarded are taught to swim should be organized and conducted so nothing is left to chance--tend the smallest detail, maintain a business-like but friendly atmosphere, and *consider the individual student all-important*. Every student needs to be accepted as an individual of worth and dignity; opportunities for each individual to derive personal satisfaction, enjoyment, and fun need to be integral parts of the instructional swimming program.

Instructors and aides soon discover the mentally retarded are more like their non-retarded peers and contemporaries than they are different; problems encountered in teaching both groups are much the same. More variation and deviation are found among classifications of mentally retarded than between the retarded and non-retarded as groups! Since the retarded are more like the non-retarded than they are different, similarities--not differences--should be reflected in programs, including instructional swimming. Many innovative, creative, and unusual approaches and activities[1] have been developed to meet specific needs of some mentally retarded individuals and groups. These same methods and techniques can be as effective--if not more so--with other groups having like needs, exhibiting similar problems in learning to swim, and functioning at comparable levels. Instructors and aides must always be alert to recognize as early as possible signs of frustration, unusual behavior, and other trouble symptoms so the teaching approach and learning activities can be modified immediately.

Progressions in swimming include more than the specific sequences of instruction used in a pool or lake. In the broadest sense teaching progressions include the student's earliest experiences with water, preparing him to go to the pool for the instructional program, going to the pool, changing clothes, and showering; many factors often taken for granted with the non-retarded must be planned for, structured with, and taught to the retarded. Certain administrative details must be included when considering progressions.

Parental and medical approval must be secured before allowing an individual to take part in a swimming program.[2] Instructors should have access to all pertinent information about each student for better understanding of his abilities and disabilities, and his strengths and weaknesses. Prior to the first instructional session, instructors need to obtain information about each student's background, experience, and interest in swimming and aquatic activities.

This information is valuable in determining a student's readiness for participation and instruction; his reactions to water, to other students in the class, and to instructors and aides are further indications of his readiness for learning. A screening test or other means of evaluating a student's level of swimming ability *must* be used to determine the class or group to which he can be safely assigned. Some retardates can be enrolled immediately

---

[1]See Chapters III (Methods), V (Stunts and Games), and VII (Behavior Modification Techniques) for detailed discussion of some innovative, creative, and unusual approaches and activities for instructional and recreational swimming programs.

[2]Discussion of this topic and suggested forms are in Chapter II (Organizing and Administering the Program).

in a class with non-retarded; others will have to start in groups of four to
eight and may be reassigned to groups or classes of non-retarded when progress warrants change; still others may need continued instruction on a one-
to-one basis because of physical, psychological, emotional, or environmental
conditions.

No set pattern or approach can guarantee success with all students.
What one instructor finds successful, another will not; what is successful
with one group will not work with another group--this is particularly true
in helping students become acclimated and adjusted to water. Some instructors
find a formal and structured skill and drill approach successful at this
stage; others use an informal or play approach; some use combinations--
part formal, part informal; some structured, some unstructured; portions
drill, portions play--depending upon the progress and needs of the individual
student. Usually the retardate has to be approached in different ways to
teach and reinforce movements, skills, and strokes at various stages in the
instructional swimming program.

The instructor must be flexible, make changes and adjustments he deems
necessary for individual students, allow for modification of techniques, and
capitalize on all teachable moments. To accomplish this, the instructor
must have the courage of his convictions and be willing to break with tradition and convention when this appears in the best interests of his students.
A successful instructor can have no preconceived ideas of what the retarded
can and cannot do; he must understand swimming progressions minutely so he
can move in a direction best suited for his students. The ability to break
down skills and strokes into their basic component parts, to develop methods
and approaches to teach these fundamentals, and a willingness to experiment
and try the untried are characteristic of the successful instructor who uses
his knowledge of swimming progressions as one of his most important assets.
This is the same instructor who recognizes in his student the precise moment
when he is receptive and ready to learn a specific movement, skill, or stroke.

Orientation: Foundation for Progress

The student must feel at ease and comfortable in the area where he is to
be taught; much can be done to orient him before going to the pool or lake.
The swimming site can be the topic of informal and formal discussions; pictures, slides, or films can be shown to acquaint students with everything
about the area--locker room, shower room, deck area, swimming area itself.
The instructor can walk with students through the area, show them what has
been included in audiovisual presentations, and talk about different areas--
the shallow end, buoys, deep water, diving board, overflows, and other
features of the pool and pool site. In this way students can become thoroughly acquainted with the facilities and are more likely to feel secure,
comfortable, and happy.

The student needs an opportunity to get the feel of water on his skin--
and on all parts of his body--hands, feet, legs, arms, face, neck, chest,
abdomen, and back. Gradually he can immerse more of his body and then walk,

run, jump, hop, gallop, and skip across the pool. Students can take giant steps across the pool, count their steps between designated points, increase or decrease the size of their steps, and race across the pool to become more at home in water. Selected games and relays can be valuable at this stage to promote water acclimation and adjustment. When the student feels relaxed and comfortable in the water he may be introduced to breath control activities--blowing bubbles, rhythmic breathing, bobbing, and games in which he goes under water.

An orientation series[3] appropriate for trainable mentally retarded and adaptable to the timid and the young should include--

1. *This Is the Way We Wash Our Face*--use the song and motions to help students adjust to temperature and feel of water, and then to immerse their hair, face, arms, and torso in that order.

2. *Lions' Roar*--roar like a lion and then place face in water; forceful roaring insures that the student blows bubbles.

3. *Motor Boat Races*--walk across the pool doing the Lions' Roar. Make sure students exhale before taking another breath as a preliminary to immersing the face and rhythmic breathing.

4. *Ring Around the Rosie*--get students to immerse completely while doing Lions' Roar. Stress exhalation under water to discourage students from inhaling under water and to reinforce principles of rhythmic breathing.

5. *Blow Out Candles*--have student blow out a candle and then repeat to further his concepts of rhythmic breathing. Have him come up from under water, open his eyes, blow out candles, and go back under water. Ask him how many candles he blew out at one time which will encourage him to keep his eyes open.

6. *Picking Posies*--use pucks for posies and see if students can pick them off the bottom of the pool; make sure students keep their eyes open.

Some instructors have found an extended period of orientation and conditioning to water, including games, races, stunts, relays, and similar pool activities, facilitates instruction in later stages because of greater confidence and the secure feeling in water developed by students.

----

[3]Adapted from material submitted by Gary Muehlhauson, Brainerd State Hospital, Brainerd, Minnesota.

Breath Control and Breathing

Breath control and breathing in water need to be stressed in all phases of an instructional swimming program. However, some instructors who have been successful in teaching the mentally retarded to swim disagree as to *when* breathing should be introduced. Some advocate teaching breath control and breathing before teaching the prone float or glide, while others insist that breath control and breathing should not be attempted before propulsion skills have been developed. Both groups offer sound reasons and a logical rationale for their positions. On the one hand, if breath control and breathing are learned before the prone float or glide, they can be used by students as they learn other movements, skills, and strokes so that coordinating this skill--breathing--with others may create fewer learning problems. On the other hand, if students are able to move and propel themselves prior to being concerned with breath control and breathing, they can concentrate on this single skill at the appropriate time as they develop a specific stroke. The fact that instructors have found both approaches, as well as combinations of the two, successful, reflects the individuality of learning and the necessity for approaching each student in ways to which he is most receptive and which are successful with him.

Regardless of approaches taken relative to breath control and breathing, instructors must be ready to provide instruction in this vital area with each of the various stages and in each of the different positions discussed in the following sections. Breathing is discussed as it relates to floating in various positions and to propelling one's self through the water in different positions. Instructors and aides will soon learn the most feasible, practical, and effective approach to take regarding breath control and breathing in water for each of their students.

Floating

A variety of sequences and approaches are often necessary to teach a retarded student to float. Floating positions are basic to develop the feel and concept of buoyancy. Many students fail to realize water is their friend and will help them stay afloat if they relax and take it easy; when whipped and fought, water is no friend, fights back and may drag them down. Buoyancy is fundamental to moving in water and learning to recover from various horizontal positions; this introduces him to a basic aquatic survival skill. Included in the progressions of floating are:

1. *Orientation to Floating.* The group or class is seated at the edge of the shallow end of the pool with the instructor and an assistant (demonstrator) in waist-deep water. The instructor explains that his *buddy* will float while holding onto a balloon! The demonstrator blows up the balloon and holds it with both hands, extended to assist in a prone float. The instructor points out that the air which went into the balloon came from the balloons--lungs--inside his assistant's chest. In other words, get enough air in your lungs and you will be able to float.

77

2. *Alligator Position.* This method is appropriate only in pools
    where the water depth is between 12 and 24 inches so the stu-
    dent's hands can safely reach the bottom of the pool. From
    the basic alligator position the student walks forward and
    backward to obtain a feeling of buoyancy in water; moves on
    his elbows with his head out of water; holds his breath and
    places his face in the water; walks in the alligator posi-
    tion with his head in the water; attempts to lift both hands
    to the surface simultaneously while keeping his face in the
    water; goes into a prone float from a half kneeling position.
    As a student gains skill, proficiency, and confidence, he
    should be encouraged and challenged to perform each of these
    activities for longer periods of time.

3. *Basic Face Down Floats.* *Jelly Fish and Turtle* are two basic
    face down floats which may help a student improve his sense
    of balance in water, develop a feeling of buoyancy, and build
    confidence.

    In the *Jelly Fish Float* the student stands in waist-deep
    water with his feet apart. He bends at the waist, places
    the hands on his thighs, inhales through the mouth, places
    his face in water, and slides the hands down toward his
    ankles. When he grasps his ankles the entire body will
    float like a jelly fish. Procedures are reversed for the
    recovery--slide hands back toward the thighs, lift the
    face out of water, and exhale through the mouth.

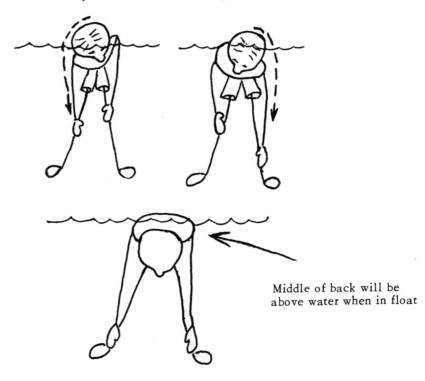

Middle of back will be
above water when in float

78

In the *Turtle Float*, the student also stands in waist-deep
water with the feet apart. He bends forward at the waist,
places both hands on one thigh, inhales through the mouth,
lowers the face in water, and slowly slides both hands down
the leg to a position just below this knee which is pulled
to the chest and held for a predetermined count. Recovery
is accomplished by lowering the leg, sliding the hands up
to the thigh, raising the face from the water, and exhaling.
The same procedures are repeated for the other leg and then
both legs together.

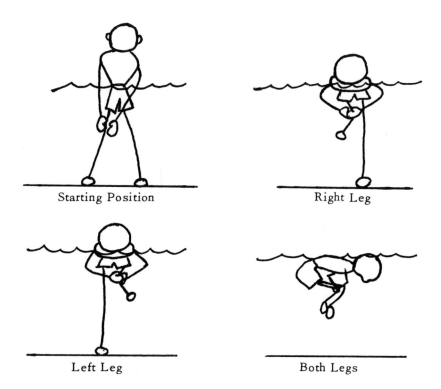

Starting Position   Right Leg

Left Leg   Both Legs

4. *Back Float and Recover to a Stand*. Often the back float is
    introduced by getting the student in proper position and
    supporting his head on the instructor's shoulder. This frees
    the instructor's hands to position the student's body and
    makes for a good position for communication between the two.
    The instructor can talk encouragingly and confidently to the
    student. As the student relaxes and gains confidence the in-
    structor can lower his shoulder so the student uses less
    support and floats more on his own. However, the shoulder
    is always there when assistance is needed. This is an ef-
    fective way to work with small children in chin-deep water.

Another approach helpful at this stage is to have an aide
hold the student's feet and legs while the instructor holds
the back of the student's head and supports his upper torso.
This helps the student get the feel of the proper position
for the back float. Basic considerations of proper back
float positions include: keep the head well back in the
water, hold the arms under water, keep the hips at the
surface of the water, push the abdomen up slightly, and
lift the hands clear of the water by bending at the wrist
if the feet sink too far.

Many retardates will not move their feet off the bottom of
the pool when they start the back float from a standing
position. However, as the student feels his torso supported
he often raises his feet voluntarily. Initially, the instructor may have to support the student's torso by holding his back and having him touch only his heels to the
bottom of the pool. Generally from this position the student lifts his heels and legs and moves on his own toward
an unassisted back float position. In all cases gradually
lessen physical support of the instructor so the student
develops a greater sense of success and independence. The
instructor can give the student problems to solve as in
movement exploration,[4] which often speeds up the learning
process and makes learning more permanent through self-
discovery.

Recovery is accomplished by bringing the arms down to the
sides in a sweeping arc as if pulling a chair under you.
As the knees are bent and brought back toward the chest,
a forward roll action results which brings the face forward; drop the chin to the chest and assist the roll
action. When the face is almost in the water, the legs
should be extended by thrusting the feet to the bottom
of the pool to regain a standing position.

<hr />

[4] See pages 66-70 for a detailed discussion of movement exploration as
applied to the instructional swimming program.

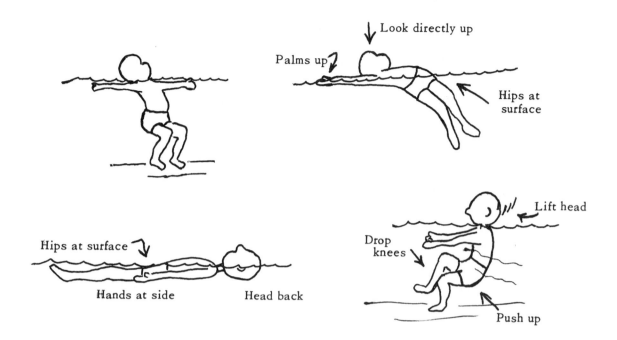

Look directly up

Palms up

Hips at surface

Hips at surface

Hands at side

Head back

Lift head

Drop knees

Push up

5. *Prone Float and Recover to a Stand*. Generally the same procedures apply in teaching the prone float and recovery as in
teaching the back float and recovery--go from the known to
the unknown, build upon previously mastered skills, use lessening amounts of support, and move to increasing water depths.
If the student has mastered the turtle float he simply extends his arms forward, hooks his thumbs, and goes into a
prone float by straightening his knees and legs. Some students will need support to assist them *develop the feel* of
a proper prone float position. Support can be given by an
instructor or aide who holds the student according to his
need, from the side of the pool or an overflow, or from a
kickboard or other assistive device. Gradually support is
decreased until the student floats by himself. Ways of
lessening support include--take one hand at a time off the
kickboard, assistive device, side of the pool, or overflow
and reduce physical support from instructor or aide. As
the student begins to float on his own encourage and challenge
him to stay afloat for longer periods of time.

Basic considerations of good form include--keep the body
straight with ears between extended arms, keep the face in
the water to stay close to the surface, to reduce any tendency to roll, spread the legs and help raise the feet by
turning up the fingers and palms of the hands. Ordinarily
palms of the hands will be down. Students also can explore

and discover what happens when they move their hands and arms
or kick their feet and legs while in this position. At this
stage there is little need to insist upon specific movement
patterns--simply encourage students to move their arms and
legs and most will attempt basic sculling, finning, and kicking skills. Some report success and enthusiastic response
from retarded students by using appealing names for various
skills--*Superman* or *Batman Float*.

Recovery is accomplished by returning to the turtle position
and then to a stand. The knees should be tucked and brought
close to the chest, arms extended and brought straight down
through the water to the side, and the head raised out of
the water in returning to a standing position. Initially
some students may need to hold the side of the pool, bring
both knees to the chin, and then place the feet on the bottom
of the pool.

Some special considerations in teaching the prone float and
recovery include--lift hands from the bottom of the pool by
balancing on the fingers so the student literally floats off
the bottom of the pool; bend elbows to lift hands away from
the bottom of the pool; roll up a medium size bath towel and
place it under the student's chin to help keep his face in
the water. In the recovery, to minimize tripping and loss
of balance, keep the face in the water until the arms are
brought down to the side of the body and the feet placed on
the bottom of the pool.

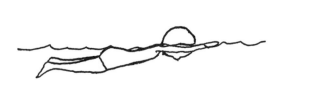 

Propulsion

All students want to feel they are swimming, so getting them to move--
to propel themselves through water--is important to them and to the success
of the program. The successful swimmer relates movements of various parts
of the body and is able to coordinate the actions of upper and lower limbs.
Swimming movements, skills, and strokes require that the arms and legs be
used independently or in various combinations--homologous or bilateral where

82

both arms or legs work together as in the breast stroke, butterfly, or elementary back stroke; homolateral where the arms and legs on the same side of the body work together as in the side stroke; cross pattern where the arms and legs on opposite sides of the body work together as in the crawl or back crawl. Students can move from the known to the unknown by adding another movement or skill to that which they already know and can perform--simply add a glide, kick, or arm movement to a float. With time and practice stressing single specific movements and skills, habits are developed which make the process of combining and coordinating these movements and skills into strokes more efficient and effective. Severely and profoundly retarded, multiply and physically handicapped youngsters can be taught to swim. Aquatic or swim patterning[5] techniques are being introduced to and successfully used with many handicapped individuals who have progressed from this simple stage to competent deep water swimmers. Aquatic patterning capitalizes upon support which comes from natural buoyant effects of water upon the body; the therapist or instructor moves the arms or legs of the patient or student through specific movements and over the complete range of motion. This approach is therapeutically oriented but has implication and application for instructional swimming programs where procedures and techniques can be adapted and applied as needed.

Basic sequences of propulsion include--

On the Back

1. *Glide*. Have student hold onto the overflow or deck of the pool with both hands, keep his head back with ears in the water, and place both feet against the wall of the pool. He removes his hands from the overflow or deck, straightens his knees, and pushes away from the wall. If a student has difficulty putting both feet against the wall of the pool, have him place one foot against the wall and the other on the bottom of the pool. As he gains confidence and skill, have him attempt the glide by squatting down as if going into a back float. From this position the student pushes back hard off the bottom so that he is gliding toward shallow water. Be sure the student stays in shallow water until he has mastered the back glide. Watch that the student does not tilt his head back too far so water will not wash back over his face. Recovery is accomplished by following the same steps as outlined for the back float.

---

[5] Contact Mrs. Judy Newman, Director, Therapeutic Swim Program, Crippled Children's Foundation, Desert Hot Springs, California, 92240, for specific information and details of aquatic or swim patterning techniques and approaches.

Push
off

2. *Kick* (with or without flotation support). Have student add
   any one of a number of kicking movements to the back glide--
   modified inverted flutter kick, inverted flutter kick, inverted scissors kick, modified inverted breast stroke kick,
   inverted breast stroke kick.

3. *Arm action* (with or without flotation support). Have student
   add any one of a number of arm movements to the back glide--
   modified finning, modified sculling, elementary back stroke
   (hands slide up the side to the armpits, arms are extended,
   and hands pulled back down to the legs), regular back crawl,
   racing back crawl. Initially emphasize strokes involving
   simple paired movements--bilateral--in which both arms make
   the same movement at the same time as in the elementary back
   stroke. The rest and glide need particular emphasis in the
   elementary back stroke. Alert the student to the possibility
   of getting a back wash of water in his face and mouth when the
   arms are moved.

4. *Combinations* of different leg and arm movements are introduced
   by adding an appropriate arm action to a given kick, or a kick
   to an effective arm movement.

5. *Breathing* should be natural and normal; little or nothing is
   said about breathing unless the student is having some particular difficulty. Generally the student inhales as the arms
   come up to the armpits and exhales as they are pulled back
   down to the legs.

In the Prone Position

1. *Glide.* Have student in waist-deep water lean forward with
   his arms extended and hands together until his shoulders
   are below the water surface. He takes a breath, places his
   face into the water, and pushes forward. The side of the
   pool can be used to add force to the glide; a kickboard or
   flutter board can be used as an aid to the student. Important considerations of good form include--keep hands and

feet together, make sure chin is down and the face is kept
under the water surface, and strive to increase distance
covered on each glide. Recovery is accomplished by following
the same steps as outlined for the prone float.

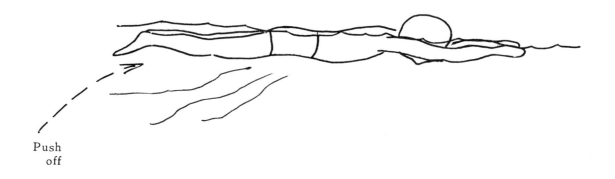

Push
off

2. *Kick* (with or without flotation support). Have student add
   any one of a number of kicking movements to the prone glide--
   slow flutter kick (probably the easiest), slow dolphin (legs
   kicked together as a unit), frog or breast stroke kick,
   scissors. Since students often try the kick which comes most
   easily and naturally to them, the instructor must watch each
   individual, diagnose and evaluate his movements, and select
   activities and methods best suited for each individual. A
   student who bends his knees excessively will often straighten
   them when he is told to keep his feet under water.

3. *Arm action* (with and without flotation support). Have student add any one of a number of arm movements to the prone
   glide. A movement frequently used at this stage is the
   human stroke--extend arms forward, pull one arm down and
   back almost to the legs, and with the elbow bent, recover
   along the side to the extended position; the arms are con-
   tinually trying to overtake one another but never quite
   successfully. (Ask students if they have ever seen a dog
   dig for a bone!) Other arm movements which may be attempted
   include--crawl, butterfly, and breast stroke. An aid to
   proper hand position can be accomplished by asking the student if he *eats* soup with a fork or spoon!

85

4. *Combinations* of different leg and arm movements are introduced by adding an appropriate arm action to a given kick,
   or a kick to an effective arm movement.

5. *Breathing* is accomplished by having the student turn his face
   to one side as the arm on that side comes out of the water at
   the end of the recovery; have him turn his head until his
   mouth clears the water. Basic mechanics of breathing must be
   emphasized--inhale sharply while the mouth is out of the water;
   exhale forcefully while the head is in the water; turn the
   head out of the water on only one side of the body; do all of
   this rhythmically. The student should not gulp air when inhaling, not exhale too much air while his head is in the water,
   and be encouraged to open his eyes when his face is submerged.

Left arm back - *inhale*   Right arm back - *exhale*

Various approaches can be used to introduce students to the
coordinations required in proper breathing--practice movements of the head by themselves with the student standing
so that his shoulders are beneath the water or with him in
a prone position holding onto the side or deck of the pool;
add breathing to arm action and practice from a standing
position; walk across the pool executing the proper arm
and head movements. Drag the toes on the bottom of the
pool while performing appropriate actions, stress proper
coordination and relaxation at all times.

   Some instructors introduce sequences in the prone position before those
on the back; other delay any use of flotation support. Some instructors
follow one sequence from beginning to end--back float to back strokes or
prone float to prone strokes--before starting another; others include comparable skills from both sequences simultaneously--back float and prone

float; back kicks and prone kicks, arm actions on the back and in the prone position. No single pattern guarantees success with every group or in all situations. Instructors must be alert to signs of confusion and indecision on the part of students and be prepared to make necessary adjustments in sequences for individual students.

Changing Position and Direction

The mentally retarded like to respond to new and exciting challenges which have meaning and significance for them. When a student fulfills an *individual challenge* he derives the personal satisfaction of knowing he, and he alone, is responsible for this success. As the student develops the ability to propel himself in both back and prone positions he can be challenged by having to change positions while swimming--

1. *Back to Front*--while swimming on the back, the swimmer reaches across his chest with one arm, turns his head toward that side, and rolls over to the front position. Many find it fun to do this continuously in a type of *barrel roll*.

Right turn from front to back

Turn head left and drop right shoulder beginning to roll over

2. *Front to Back*--while swimming in the prone position, the swimmer rolls away from the extended arm--turns the right side under if the left arm is extended, turns the left side of the face up and away from the water, and rolls over onto his back. Some students effectively use the non-extended arm as a whip to help complete the turn to the back.

Learning to change direction while swimming is an important skill for students to develop, and is equally important for their safety. All swimmers need to learn methods of returning to positions in the pool from which they started and of avoiding collisions and other dangerous situations. Specific attention must be given to changing direction from both back and prone positions--

1. *On the Back* pull harder with one hand and arm than with the
    other hand and arm to make a big, gradual turn; pull with
    only one arm for a sharp turn.

2. *In the Prone Position* move the head in the direction of the
    turn; reach gradually with the arms in this same direction
    continuing until the turn is complete; the head leads the
    turn.

The ability to level off is an important skill for students to master
before attempting to change position and direction. Leveling off should be
practiced in a variety of situations and under many different conditions--
jelly fish to turtle float, back to prone float, vertical to horizontal
float, glides from the side of the pool, after jumping into the pool, and
after a surface dive.

Instructors hope every student will develop sufficient skill and competency to become a deep water swimmer. When the student attains reasonable
proficiency, skill, and confidence he should be introduced to deep water.
Many times it is necessary to take a student through transitional stages to
convince him that he can swim safely in deep water.

Initially a student simply may lower himself into deep water while he
holds onto the overflow; he submerges but maintains his grip on the overflow.
Gradually he removes his hands from the overflow--one at a time if necessary--
and moves into a vertical float. Some instructors have students start in
shallow water, swim into deep water, and return to the shallow water starting
point; as the student gains skill, endurance, and confidence, the total distance covered is increased. Other instructors introduce students to deep
water by having them swim close to the side of the pool; *if the student gets
into trouble he immediately grabs the side*. As the student gains confidence
the instructor encourages him to move gradually away from the side of the
pool.

Water Entry

The student's approach and entry into water follow a logical progression
and sequence. The *safety jump* may be used initially. In the safety jump the
student jumps into the pool so that his head does not go under water. The
student places one foot forward, one backward, stretches his hands out and forward, and jumps directly into the water landing so that his legs are still
apart and the arms outstretched. Students may be encouraged to jump into chest-
deep water, push off the bottom and swim; they progress by stages into deeper
water. The porpoise series and surface diving offer additional challenges,
new skills, and serve as an introduction to head first entries.

Mastery of a head first entry into water usually progresses more gradually than a feet first entry. The seal dive offers many possibilities for
initially introducing the head first entry. The student takes prone position
near the edge of the pool and simply slides head first into the water. In

88

the next stage the student can be lowered into the water or slide into it from a 2 x 8 plank. Instructors can make this task easier or more difficult, more or less challenging by holding the end of the plank at different heights. These two activities capitalize upon the student's learning by doing--never do for him what he can do for himself!

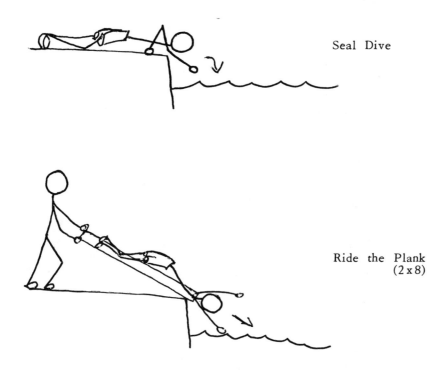

Seal Dive

Ride the Plank
(2 x 8)

Structured instruction in diving starts from a sitting position from which students move to kneeling, then standing, and finally springing. Some students must move more gradually and have sub-steps between each of the basic positions. In each position emphasize extending the arms so they lead and enter the water first; the head should be between the arms. Targets, such as tires, hoops, and inner tubes[6] can be used effectively to improve diving form. Brightly-colored weighted objects can be placed on the bottom of the pool as points of focus to help students improve diving form.

---

[6]

See page 58 for special considerations and precautions regarding use of inner tubes in swimming pools and in swimming programs.

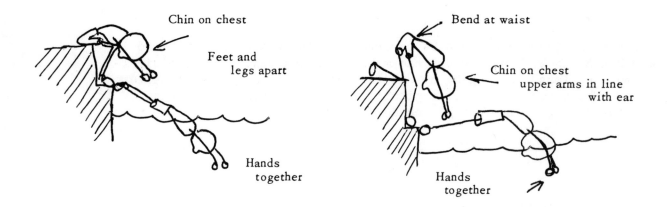

Chin on chest

Feet and
legs apart

Hands
together

Bend at waist

Chin on chest
upper arms in line
with ear

Hands
together

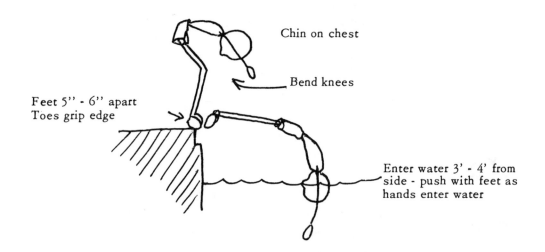

Chin on chest

Bend knees

Feet 5" - 6" apart
Toes grip edge

Enter water 3' - 4' from
side - push with feet as
hands enter water

Many instructors feel that no student should be allowed in deep water
unless he can tread water; many feel that this skill should be introduced
as soon as basic water adjustment has been made. Instructors have at their
disposal a systematic and progressive procedure to teach treading--

1. Stand in shallow water, jump up, and move the body in dif-
    ferent ways--twist, pedal as on a bike, turn.

2. Stand in waist-deep water and move the hands in various
    ways--scull, paddle, fin, wing.

3. Hold onto the overflow or deck of the pool and move the
    legs in different ways--frog kick, scissors kick, flutter
    kick, pedaling movements, or free kicking movements.

4. Hold onto the overflow or deck of the pool with one hand
    so that the opposite arm and leg can be used in a tread-
    ing motion; turn and repeat the same action with the
    other arm and leg. Encourage the student to let go of
    the wall and tread for increasing lengths of time on his own.

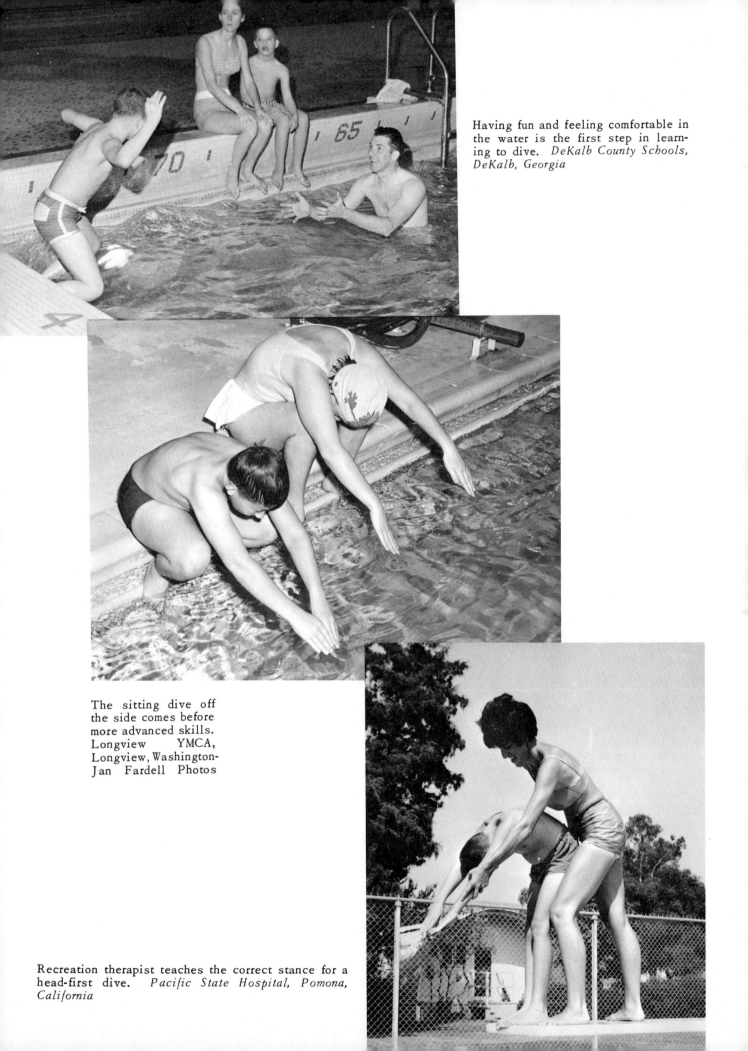

Having fun and feeling comfortable in the water is the first step in learning to dive. *DeKalb County Schools, DeKalb, Georgia*

The sitting dive off the side comes before more advanced skills. Longview YMCA, Longview, Washington-Jan Fardell Photos

Recreation therapist teaches the correct stance for a head-first dive. *Pacific State Hospital, Pomona, California*

Diving class of a teenage boys having a competitive race across the pool. *Lou Castel, Pacific State Hospital, Pomona, California*

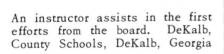An instructor assists in the first efforts from the board. DeKalb, County Schools, DeKalb, Georgia

5. Place a cane, hoop, or rope under the student's armpits for support; he moves his arms and legs through treading motions. Gradually lessen support and move to increasing depths.

6. Hold the student under his armpits or by the waist so he can make free movements with his arms and legs and progress to treading actions; gradually lessen the amount of support.

Safety

Safety, watermanship skills, survival techniques, and drownproofing must be stressed throughout all stages of the instructional program. Students should be made aware of ways in which they can help a swimmer in trouble--extend a hand or leg while holding onto support; push a supporting object while holding onto the other end; throw a line, lifebuoy, or other floating object; use a shepherd's crook, reaching pole, or towel; yell and/ or send someone for additional help. Students need planned and structured opportunities to handle flotation equipment, to use various types of life jackets, and to react to falling into the water partially or fully dressed. The importance of keeping the eyes open to orient one's self in the water, to promote better balance, provide security, and aid in comfort should be constantly emphasized. Students must be made aware of their own strengths and limitations in situations where they must help others in trouble.

Basic drownproofing procedures[7] include--

1. Take a deep breath, float face down with the chin on the chest, arms and legs dangling, and the back of the neck and shoulders at the surface of the water; hold this position for four or five seconds.

2. Draw up the arms slowly to form an *X* at the face; slowly press the arms downward until they are straight, and at the same time raise the face out of the water to blow out and take in air--*relax*.

3. Place the face back into the water, raise the arms to the *X* position, press the arms downward again and *relax*; hold for four or five seconds. The arm pressure will bring body back to the surface if there is any tendency to sink.

4. Scissor kick the legs at the same time the arms are moved if necessary to stay near the surface of the water.

---

[7]See Fred Lanoue, *Drownproofing: A New Technique for Water Safety*, Englewood Cliffs, N.J: Prentice-Hall, Inc., 1963.

Boys learn lifesaving skills with shepherd's crook, as well as swimming and diving. *Pacific State Hospital, Pomona, California*

In Conclusion

Expose students to additional styles and strokes of swimming according to their readiness, progress, and interest. Demonstrations, pageants, competition, games, and other interesting and motivating activities should be planned for and included at any stage in the complete instructional swimming program for the mentally retarded. Introduce students to small craft safety by bringing boats right into the pool.

There is no single best order or sequence to insure success in teaching every mentally retarded student to swim. Some instructors have reported a great deal of success by starting trainables on a corrupted butterfly! Analysis of the butterfly discloses a stroke neurologically more primitive and mechanically simpler to execute and coordinate than the conventional crawl. Both arms work as a unit, coming forward together and going back together; the legs are kicked as a single unit; the head may be kept out of the water at all times. The necessity for exact timing and coordination is not nearly so great and the student can progress even when he thrashes and fights the water. Student individuality precludes establishing definite progressions and time sequences which dictate when a student should move from one movement, skill, or stroke to another. Individual lesson plans and timetables need to be prepared for each student. Conventional procedures where everyone is doing the same thing for the same length of time during each swimming lesson is antiquated and has contributed much to the failures encountered in teaching the mentally retarded to swim. *The instructor must think, evaluate, diagnose, and prescribe; he has to be creative, find new devices, try fresh methods, and use approaches which will appeal to and are effective with the retarded.* In many ways teaching the retarded is like teaching the non-retarded except many times it is done in slow motion!

Thanks and appreciation are extended to the Rehabilitation Services Staff Pacific State Hospital, Pomona, California, Mrs. Frances Grove, Supervisor, for permission to use diagrams and extract materials from the Pacific State Hospital *Swimming Manual* for inclusion in this Chapter.

Junior Waterbug Progressions

1. Adjust to water.

2. Get into pool properly.

3. Get out of pool properly.

4. Sit on edge and kick.

5. Walk across pool with help.

6. Walk across pool alone.

7. Walk across pool blowing bubbles.

8. Jump like a bunny across pool.

9. Float on front with help.

10. Float on back with help.

11. Pull on front while kicking.

12. Pull on back while kicking.

13. Walk across pool with human arm stroke.

14. Human stroke with help.

15. Jump in with help.

16. Jump in 5 times alone.

17. Play water games with other children.

18. Kick across with kickboard.

19. Learn to use fins.

20. Open eyes under water.

Based on Waterbug Progressions, YMCA, Longview, Washington

Waterbug No. 1 Progressions

1. Get in the pool properly.

2. Get out of the pool properly.

3. Blows bubbles well.

4. Walk across with no help.

5. Walk across with face in water.

6. Human kick with help to ten counts.

7. Flutter kick with help to ten counts.

8. Eyes open under water.

9. Human arm stroke with help.

10. Crawl arm stroke with help.

11. Bob slowly 5 times.

12. Float on back with help and recover.

13. Jump in with help.

14. Front glide and recover.

15. Jump in 5 times alone.

16. Jump in alone getting head under.

17. Walk across with human arm stroke and face in water.

18. Water bug float on front alone for 5 counts.

19. Bob slowly 10 times.

20. Pick object off bottom.

21. Water bug sitting dive.

22. Swim alone at all.

23. Water bug float on back alone 5 counts.

24. Flutter kick on back with help 10 counts.

25. Wing on the back alone for 10 counts.

26. Bob with rhythmic breathing.

27. Water bug diving glide.

28. Swim 5 strokes alone any combination.

29. Swim under water one body length.

30. Cork float count of 5.

31. Flutter back scull to 10 counts.

32. Swim across pool alone.

33. Roll from front to back.

Waterbug No. 2 Progressions

Skills must be executed in deep water unless indicated otherwise.

1. Duck down to bottom facing wall and back up.

2. Tread water using one of the following kicks: scissors, frog, flutter or whip, for one minute.

3. Jellyfish float for 10 counts.

4. Back float horizontal 10 counts.

5. Back float balanced 10 counts.

6. Back float vertical 10 counts.

7. Jumping surface dive in chest deep water.

8. Jump off diving board and swim to the side.

9. Jump in, level off, swim 20 ft.

10. Change positions.

11. Change directions.

12. Bob 10 times with one breath between each bob.

13. Standing dive, swim 20 ft., turn on top of water, swim back. (perfect form not required.

14. Steamboat, width of pool.

15. Back float and frog kick across pool.

16. Elementary back arm stroke only across pool.

17. Three porpoise dives across the pool.

18. Kneeling dive off board.

19. Jump in, swim 20 ft., reverse direction and return on back.

20. Standing front dive.

21. Elementary back stroke, width of pool.

22. Flutter pack scull pool width.

23. Plunge dive and under water swim 15 ft.

24. Duck down to bottom, swim under water across pool.

25. Front crawl with *rhythmic breathing* across pool.

26. Survival swim 1 minute.

Waterbug No. 3 Progressions

1. Change position (front to back)

2. Change position (back to front)

3. Practice assist with pole and wading human chain.

4. Flutter kick on front across pool.

5. Flutter kick on back across pool.

6. Side stroke (arms & legs) across pool.

7. Breast stroke (arms & legs) across pool.

8. Use ring buoy (throw, heaving line) tow someone using kickboard.

9. Elementary back stroke across pool.

10. Back float in deep water. (1 Min.)

11. Scull on back (hands at side) across pool.

12. Feet first **scull** across pool.

13. Stay afloat in one spot 30 sec.

14. Overarm side stroke (2 times to rope and back)

15. Tread water, scissors kick one minute.

16. Underwater swim across pool.

17. Running jump from low elevation (enter with feet together)

18. Standing front dive from board.

19. Swim in place for 5 min. no touch--sides or bottom.

20. Swim 2 lengths of pool using not more than two different strokes.

Special Skills (optional)

1. Simple synchronized swimming skills.
2. Survival swimming.
3. Use life jacket.
4. Life saving jump.

Waterbug No. 4 Progressions

1. Side stroke (60 Yds.) with proper turns.

2. Elementary back (60 Yds.).

3. Crawl stroke (60 Yds.) with proper turns.

4. Back crawl (20 Yds.).

5. On back, legs only (40 Yds.) inverted scissors or breast kick.

6. Corkscrew swim to the rope.

7. Torpedo swim across pool.

8. Jack Knife (pike) surface dive in 8 ft. water and swim 3 body lengths.

9. Tuck surface dive in 8 ft. water and swim 3 body lengths.

10. Feet first surface dive in 8 ft. water and swim 3 body lengths.

11. Long shallow dive (racing or starting dive).

12. Feet first entry into deep water (feet together).

13. Jump from low board.

14. Standing dive from low board.

15. Back dive from low board.

16. Swim 6 lengths using two strokes.

17. Dive in - glide or swim under water to rope.

18. Tread water for 5 minutes.

19. Front turn - crawl, breast stroke and side stroke. (Do one of three).

20. Swim with clothes on - disrobe and use clothes for support.

21. Practice with life jacket.

22. Lifesaving jump.

23. Swim in a line and in a circle.

24. Wrist tow and extension tow.

Swimming Progressions

Group Activities

Sits on edge of pool and kicks in water.

Enjoys being carried about in water.

Permits teacher to sprinkle him with water.

Permits self to be doused with water.

Stands in water.

Stands in water splashing with hands.

Talks in Pool.

Plays game squatting up to neck for *fall down*

Puts face in water holding on to teacher.

Plays game going under water for *fall down.*

Individual Activities

Allows self to be held in prone position.

Kicks when held or towed in prone position.

Makes arm movements when held in prone position.

Stands up from prone position.

Puts face in water.

Blows bubbles.

Glides in prone position.

Kicks in prone position by self.

Makes arm and leg movements in prone position by self.

Breathe while in motion.

Swims width of pool.

Opportunity School, Noblesville, Indiana

Swimming Skills and Progressions

Skills

Approach water

Enter water

Walk to shoulder deep water

Hold Breath

Blow out

Face in water

Blow Bubbles

Bobbing

Jump into waist deep water

Kick holding onto flutter board

Prone float

Recovery to standing position

Front tow with kick

Kick holding onto stationary
   object

Prone glide

Front arm pull

Rhythmic breathing

Human stroke

Back float

Recover to standing position

Back glide

Back tow with kick

Kick on back

Finning and combined back stroke

Turning over from front to back

Swim for distance – front and back

Changing direction

Swim in deep water

Tread water

Jump in deep water

Dive from side

Dive from spring board

Games

Opportunity School, Noblesville, Indiana

YMCA SWIMMING PROGRESSIONS

1. Adjustment to water
   --jump from side of pool
   --exhaling under water   --*Drylander*
2. Holding breath
3. Dive from side of pool

4. Ride, glide on front
5. Ride, glide on front and regain feet.   --*Amoeba*
6. Flutter kick

7. Dive, glide, and kick
   --change directions
8. Crawl arm pull   --*Guppie*
9. Butterfly arm pull (without
   legs)

10. Crawl arm pull with kick
11. Butterfly pull with crawl
    kick   --*Tadpole*
12. Dive, swim 25 feet with
    crawl pull and kick

13. Buoyancy float
14. Recover object
15. Surface dive
16. Underwater swim
17. Back float ten feet
18. Standing dive into deep   --*Minnow*
    water
19. Safety swim
20. Change to resting stroke
21. Combination swim in deep
    water

Wilmington YMCA, Wilmington, Delaware

SWIMMING ACHIEVEMENT RECORD

This is to certify that

_____

participated in the Beginning Swimming Class

held — Date

Instructor _____

Pool _____

Name _____

PARK & RECREATION DEPARTMENT

122.01—32

BREATH HOLDING	☐		☐	COMBINED STROKE (FRONT)
RHYTHMIC BREATHING	☐	**PARK & RECREATION DEPARTMENT**	☐	COMBINED STROKE (BACK)
PRONE FLOAT	☐	**SWIMMING CHECK LIST**	☐	CHANGE OF DIRECTION
PRONE GLIDE	☐		☐	TURNING OVER
BACK FLOAT	☐		☐	LEVELING OFF
BACK GLIDE	☐		☐	JUMP (INTO WAIST DEEP WATER)
KICK GLIDE (FRONT)	☐			
KICK GLIDE (BACK)	☐		☐	JUMP (INTO DEEP WATER)
			☐	PLAIN FRONT DIVE
ARM STROKE	☐		☐	SCULLING

STUNTS AND GAMES APPLIED TO SWIMMING PROGRAMS FOR THE MENTALLY RETARDED

Ready for a group game. *Longview YMCA, Longview, Washington*

Anyone who has taught the mentally retarded to swim realizes the need and importance of a diversified program; the successful program includes many different approaches in presenting a variety of activities. Classes in which an instructor does nothing but yell, "Kick! Kick! Pull! Pull!" get pretty dull and monotonous for both students and instructors. The good swimming instructor has many games and stunts at his disposal which can be adapted for group and individual use.

Stunts and games can serve two major purposes--(1) to acclimate the beginner in a pleasant and satisfying manner to water so his first ventures into water are a personal joy and triumph which will encourage him to continue; (2) to give incentive to the good swimmer to improve and to provide him additional satisfaction as he masters more difficult stunts, games, and skills. Stunts and games can provide activity in beginning, intermediate, and advanced swimming classes which in many instances will be remembered and enjoyed more than formal approaches to learning swimming skills. A class interspersed with stunts and games can be more interesting, motivating, and stimulating than a completely formal program.

This compilation of water stunts and games has been adapted from one originally prepared and issued in 1946 for use by Red Cross field representatives and water safety instructors in the Southeastern area. No pretense is made that this listing is original; acknowledgement is freely given all available sources--known and unknown--which have been drawn upon in developing this listing. No attempt has been made to be exhaustive in listing stunts and games; this is simply a sampling of various activities as they can and have been adapted to swimming programs for the mentally retarded. Instructors and aides are referred to elementary school physical education stunts and games books[1] for additional activities of this type which can be adapted to swimming programs for the mentally retarded. Stunts and games with which the student is already familiar are particularly good since they involve only the change from land to water--the youngster already knows the basis of the activity. The resourceful instructor will modify these activities and add to the collection according to the needs, abilities, and limitations of students in his situation.

Stunts and games have been classified according to level of swimming skill. There is, of course, much overlap in classifying this way since many stunts and games listed for swimmers can be adapted and modified by using them in shallow water or adjusting the pattern for non-swimmers. When appropriate, notations are included with particular stunts or games so they can be applied directly to teaching specific skills or movements. In many instances interest, proficiency and enthusiasm can be increased by performing many of these activities to appropriate music.

Games for Beginners

The following games are particularly adaptable for non-swimmers--beginning level. Always consider the individual in choosing games--start him out gently and gradually progress into activities requiring additional activity and increased submersion.

---

[1]Several elementary school stunts and games books are listed in the bibliography of this publication.

Counting Fingers

Have children divide into pairs--one child ducks under water while the other child remains in a standing position and extends any number of fingers under water so the submerged partner can see them. As soon as the latter counts the fingers, he stands up and checks with his partner to see if he is correct. The other child then submerges and counts fingers.

Walking Race

Line the class up on one side of the shallow end of the pool. On the command, "Begin!" each student walks as fast as he can through the water to the opposite side of the pool--the first to arrive wins the race. Other basic movements (run, jump, hop, gallop) can be substituted for walking.

Leap Frog

Line players up in shallow water--last student in line puts his hands on shoulders of student in front of him, pushes latter under water and leaps over him with feed spread wide. Continue in this manner until student first in line becomes last. This is a good game to help students feel *at home in water*.

Keep Away

Choose sides and play in the shallow end of the pool. The object of the game is for one side to keep a ball away from the other team. This game may be adapted for swimmers and played in the deep end of the pool.

Fox and Ducks

Choose a player to be the Fox and another to be Mother Duck. Other students are little ducks who form a line behind Mother Duck with each holding the waist of the one in front of him. The Fox attempts to catch the last duck--the line led by Mother Duck turns in various ways to protect the last little duck from being caught by the Fox. When the last duck is tagged, he becomes Fox and Fox becomes Mother Duck.

Dodge Ball

(This game is particularly enjoyed by youngsters and they do learn to duck!) Choose sides and play in the shallow end of the pool; group one forms a large circle around group two. Students forming the outside circle have one or two volleyballs or water polo balls with which they attempt to hit players in the middle of the circle--those within the circle may walk, run, dodge, duck under the water, or swim to avoid being hit. As soon as a player is hit with the ball, he takes his place on the outer circle and assists in hitting players within the circle. When all players have been hit, the groups change places and the procedure is repeated. The last two players hit in a game may be designated captains for the next contest. An interesting variation of this game is to check the length of time it takes each team to eliminate the other; when a student is hit, he is out--the team taking *least* time to hit all opposing players wins.

Splash

Line students up in two rows about four feet apart and splash water with the palm of the hand towards the other line. The line that sticks longest wins. This is a good warm-up game.

Squirrels in Trees

Divide class into groups of three; two students in each group join hands while third student (squirrel) stands enclosed in the arms of the tree. One or two students, treeless squirrels, move among the trees. On signal, trees raise their branches (arms), and squirrels move out. All squirrels then try to get to trees; those not successful move through water until next signal when process is repeated. Periodically rotate squirrels and trees so all have opportunities to participate in each position. Specific movements can be required of squirrels--walk, run, jump, hop, gallop, go under water, surface dive.

Spinning Top

Draw the knees up against the chest, keep the hips down, and spin around on own axis by sculling with hands below the body; push water forward with the right hand and backward with the left.

Third Frog in the Puddle

Form a double circle with couples facing each other in the shallow end of the pool; choose one student to be *it* and one to be chased. The chased may walk or swim around or between players and is free from being tagged when he stands between two players of any group; then the one who is *it* must attempt to tag the student towards whom the chased player turned his back. The one who is tagged becomes *it* and should try to tag the one who caught him. Short and quick changes are necessary to make the game exciting.

Simon Says

Have players stand in waist or chest-deep water and face the leader who calls out skills to be performed. Some commands are prefaced with "Simon says," and others called out without "Simon says;" students are to perform only skills that "Simon says" to do. Players moving at the wrong time may be eliminated from the game or may acquire points against them so that the individual with the highest number of points loses and the one with the lowest number wins. Some skills for "Simons says" include blowing bubbles, jelly-fish float, treading water, ducking the head, and touching the button.

Number Retrieve

(Beginners can play Number Retrieve in waist-deep water, while more skilled swimmers can play in deeper water.) Have players form a circle and count off so each player has a number. The leader calls a number and simultaneously throws a slow sinking object into the center of the circle; the player whose number is called must retrieve the object before it reaches the bottom. Number Retrieve can be played for points or on a time basis.

Number Change

Assign each student a number and have the group form a circle in chest-deep water. *It* stands in the center of the circle and calls out two numbers; players assigned these numbers attempt to exchange places. *It* attempts to take one of the vacated places before the student whose number has been called gets there--the player left out of the circle becomes *it*.

Poison

Have students form a circle and each join hands with the person next to him; *poison* is some floating object anchored in the center of the circle. The group tries to pull the circle and force some player to touch *poison* while each player tries to keep from touching *poison* himself. When a player touches *poison* he is eliminated; the player remaining in the game after all others are eliminated wins. Students may grasp an endless rope instead of each other's hands.

Follow the Leader

(The abilities of the students should determine the type of activity chosen by the *leader* and the area of the pool used.) Choose a leader who selects activities everyone must perform in a given order. The leader may have an assigned number of turns or amount of times so everyone has an opportunity to be the leader. If a winner is desired, a player who fails to perform a skill has a point scored against him so the student with the lowest score wins. A variation is *add on* where one student performs a skill, the next does this plus one he adds, and so on. This can be done by students individually or simultaneously.

Space Formations

Play this game with one small group or as a contest among several small groups competing as teams; each group has a home base. The leader calls out a formation--for beginners in shallow water, circles, columns, lines, squares, and the like, are suitable; for advanced swimmers in deep water, those same formations plus letters or numbers may be used as swimmers tread water. As soon as the formation is announced, teams move into the designated configuration; the team that assumes the correct formation first wins a point. After the point has been awarded, teams return home. This game may be played for a certain number of points or on a time basis.

Treasure Hunt

Sink or float a variety of objects in the playing area, assign various objects different point values. For example, a puck may be worth one point, a flipper worth five points, and a ten pound weight ten points. Two teams are stationed equidistant from the playing area; on the starting signal players go into the playing area and retrieve as many objects as they can as quickly as possible. After a specified time of *treasure hunting,* the value of the *loot* of each side is counted--the team with the most points wins.

Group Games--Shallow Water

Many favorite land games can make specific contributions to swimming programs for the mentally retarded. Students have enjoyed these familiar activities in other situations so they are less conscious and aware of the water. These games can be used effectively to promote water orientation and acclimation, develop basic readiness skills, and encourage specific movements in the water. The group situation often results in the student succeeding in activities he would not otherwise attempt by himself and at the same time this can be an effective way to promote social awareness and consciousness by the retarded.

Bull in the Ring

Have students form a circle and each join hands with the person next to him. *Bull* in the center of the circle tries to break through the circle.

Cat and Mouse

Have students form a circle; two students, one a *Cat* and the other a *Mouse,* remain out of the circle. Cat chases the Mouse; students on the circle help Mouse and hinder Cat.

Polo Ball Hustle

Have students form two lines and pass a ball over their heads, like in relays.

Over and Under

Have teams form columns in chest-deep water with all students facing the same direction. On the starting signal, the last person in each team leap-frogs over the person directly in front of him, then goes between the legs of the next person in line; leapfrogs the next, goes under the next, continuing in this manner. The new person at the end of the line starts immediately after the person who starts behind him goes through the legs of the one

in front of him. The team getting all of its members to the designated line
first wins.

Hokey Pokey

Follow instructions and movements of folk dance performed on land.
Develop variations and movements according to level, ability, and interest
of group; swimming skills and activities can be substituted for traditional
movements of *Hokey Pokey*. Use other folk and square dance activities in
this same manner.

Tunnel Swim

Divide 8 to 20 players into two teams; have the members of each team
stand single file in the shallow end of the pool. Players, with the exception
of the last one in line, stand with feet spread wide apart. On the word "Go",
the last player in each line swims under water between the legs of other players to the front of the line. When he reaches the front of the line, he stands
and spreads his feet apart. The player who is now last in line watches carefully, and when the first swimmer's head appears above the water at the front
of the line begins his underwater swim. Each player has a turn so when the
game is finished players will be lined up in the same order as at the beginning
of the game.

Fish and Net

Have half the class join hands in circle formation to make a *net* in
which they try to catch the other members of the class who are the *fish*.
Hands must remain joined while catching fish; as they are caught, fish become part of the net. The last fish to be caught is the winner. Teams reverse roles for the next game.

Shallow Water Races

These simple races are wonderful devices for making the student feel at
home in the water. Many of these activities can be incorporated into the program for individuals or small groups as well as in race form.

Backward Walking

Walk backward (forward, sideways) through water. Let student hold his
hands in various positions to help movement through the water.

Basket Shooting

Use a water polo ball, rubber ball, volleyball, or basketball to shoot
baskets (play Horse, Around the World, or similar basketball lead-up games).
A round basket with the bottom knocked out and nailed to some portable support
makes an excellent basket if regulation ones are not installed in the pool or
swimming site.

Crawl

Go under water and crawl through spread feet of a partner, instructor, or aide.

Hopping

Hop (one foot then the other), jump, skip, gallop, run through water. Let student hold his hands in various positions to help movement through the water. Many basic movements, non-locomotor as well as locomotor, can be incorporated into aquatic activities.

Cork Retrieve

Divide the class into two teams; the instructor throws several handfuls of corks into the water, gives a signal, and the teams recover as many corks as possible. The team collecting the greater number of corks at the end of a designated period of time wins.

Outboard-Motor Race

Give a kickboard to each swimmer or to each team; student holds kickboard with both hands. Each player or the first member of each team kicks to the goal or to the second player, who kicks back continuing in this manner until all have had turns. The individual or team that finishes first wins.

Motionless Floating

Assume a face float position--extend arms over head, hold breath, blow out all the air through the nose in a steady stream and try to sink to the bottom of the pool. Usually the student slides down and back toward his feet. Lie flat on the bottom (face down) for a moment, place one or both feet on the bottom (or simply both hands), and spring to the surface.

Games For Beginners and Intermediate Swimmers

The majority of these games are readily adaptable for both beginner and intermediate levels. Included are tag games which seem to have universal appeal since the joy of pursuit appears to be a basic human urge, especially among children at certain age and developmental levels. The alert instructor can adapt, modify, and improvise so most of these activities can be used in almost any situation. Many of the tag games can be played in a variety of ways according to student needs and abilities.

Chinese Tag

Have *it* chase and try to tag other players. The one tagged becomes *it* who must touch the spot on the body tagged while he chases others.

Plain Tag

Have *it* chase and try to tag other players who try to avoid being tagged by moving through the water.

Under-Water Tag

Have *it* chase and try to tag other players. The player being tagged and the one tagging must both be underwater before the one tagged becomes *it*. A variation is to play so that the player being chased is safe from becoming *it* when he is completely underwater.

Cross Tag

Have *it* designate another player whom he chases. The one being chased becomes *it* if he is tagged. When another player moves between the one being chased and *it*, the one moving between them becomes the player to be chased.

Ostrich Tag

Have players close together in one end, preferably the shallow end, of the pool; one student is designated to be *it* who chases the others until someone is tagged. To keep from becoming *it* when tagged, a player must have one arm under one leg and hold his nose between thumb and fingers of the hand which goes under the leg. A player tagged who is not in the *safe* position becomes *it*.

Will O' The Wisp ✶

(This is a good game for 10 to 15 players.) Blindfold all players with a cloth which cannot become undone easily. All go into water with *it* who is not blindfolded and who carries a cow bell or other small bell. *It* muffles the clapper at first as he rings the bell and dives under water as he does so; he remains *it* until one of the blindfolded players tags him at which time the two change places. Confine players to water to avoid possible injury outside of pool.

Hill Dill or Pom Pom Pull Away

(This game is very popular among teenage boys.) Have everyone but the person who is *it* line up on one side of the pool. When *it* calls "HILL DILL" everyone must try to cross to the other side of the pool without being tagged or caught. Whoever is tagged or caught before he touches the other side of the pool then helps *it* catch others on their return trip across the pool --continue until all are caught. This game can be made more interesting by making it necessary for players to be pulled above the water if under, or ducked under if on top, rather than merely tagging or catching them.

Ball Tag

Play in a specified area in water waist-deep for non-swimmers or in deep water for swimmers. *It* tries to *tag* someone by hitting him with a ball; the one hit becomes *it*.

Japanese Tag

Designate a certain part of the body--head, back, right shoulder, left hand, etc.--which must be tagged by *it*. Players tagged on the designated part join *it* and help tag remaining players.

Stunt Tag

Designate a certain part of the body which must be brought above water to activate the player; *it* may then tag any player who has been activated. Variations include keeping the part out of water, having parts both under and out of water, etc., to activate a player.

Handicap Tag

(This is a good conditioning game for 5 to 15 players which encourages and promotes skilled watermanship.) Designate one player as *it* who tries to tag the other players as they move about the pool; all tagging must be on arms or legs. When a player is tagged, he continues to move about the pool but cannot use the arm or leg that was tagged. A player who has been tagged several times and can no longer move at all is out of the game--the player staying in motion longest wins.

Kitty In The Water

Have players in water and touching the side of the pool; each player uses this mark or spot for his base. *It* is stationed near center of pool and tries to tag players as they exchange places with one another--player tagged becomes *it*.

Link Tag

Have *it* chase and try to tag other players; those caught join hands and chase others until all are caught.

Turtle Tag

Have *it* chase and try to tag other players who must assume tuck position to be free and not become *it* when tagged.

Swimming Spell Down

Divide players into teams and have them line-up near their side of the pool. The instructor calls out a stunt--students who perform the stunt remain in the game; others are eliminated as in a spelling bee until a champion is left. Start with easy stunts to prevent eliminating players too fast; gradually make stunts more difficult. Team competition can be incorporated into this game.

Volley Ball

Divide any number of players into two groups with one group on either side of a net which is placed so the bottom is about three feet above the water. Floating ropes with wooden beads can be used to mark the boundry lines. If possible have players rotate from shallow to deep water. Use a water polo ball and bat it with hands back and forth over net. Side failing to return ball over net or batting it over boundry lines loses ball and/or point. If side which does not serve wins the play, it gains the serve; only the serving side can score points. If serving side loses the play, it fails to score and loses the serve.

Water Basketball

Place goals according to playing area (shallow or deep water, length or width of pool apart). Play the game in water exactly as on land. Variations with one goal can be developed just as one-basket basketball. Basketball lead-up games--Twenty-one, Around the World, Horses--can be introduced for swimmers and non-swimmers alike.

Tread Tag

Designate one player as *it;* other players swim about the pool. A player must tread water to escape being tagged. *It* tries to touch a player before he stops swimming and starts to tread. A player tagged when he is not treading becomes *it.*

Log

(This is an interesting way to introduce and encourage floating practice.) Mark off spaces at opposite ends of the pool for two goals. One player, the *log,* floats on his back in the center of the pool midway between the two goals. The other players (5 to 20) swim in a circle around the *log* who without warning suddenly rolls over and chases them. Players try to reach one of the goals without being tagged by the *log;* those caught must join the *log* and float in the center with the first *log.* The last player caught becomes the first *log* for the next game.

115

Still Pond

(This is another game for 5 to 20 players to develop floating and treading skills.) Have *it* stand at one side of the pool and cover his eyes with his hands. As soon as *it* covers his eyes all other players start to swim the length of the pool. *It* counts aloud from 1 to 10, then says, "Still pond-- no more moving," and then opens his eyes. When he looks up, everyone should be floating motionless--anyone seen moving is sent back to the starting point. The game is continued until all have swum the length of the pool. Variations can include specific floats, treading, sculling, or other skills instead of motionless floating.

Games for Swimmers

While many of the following games can be adapted and modified for students of lower skill levels, the majority are most appropriate for better swimmers.

Follow the Leader

Have one student act as leader and others follow him as he performs various strokes, does different dives, and executes other swimming skills and movements in the water. Followers must do everything the leader sets for them to do; when the majority of the group can stay to the finish, its members can be rated in the human fish class.

Swimming the Duck

Divide the group into two teams, have them line up at opposite ends of the pool and place a wooden decoy duck in the center of the pool. The designated team starts for the duck on the signal; the player who gets the duck swims with it toward the opponent's goal and, if blocked, passes it (*by handing*) to a member of his team. The defensive team is credited with a *block* when one of its members secures the duck. The first team has three trials to get the duck through the *enemy lines* and to the opponent's goal. After three trials the other team gets the duck and tries to get it through to the opponent's goal. If the duck is thrown into the air, it is a *fly* and the opposing side is awarded a point. This is a strenuous game and good practice for water polo. In one variation both teams attempt to get the duck at the same time, the one getting it going on offense and the other on defense. In other variations more than one duck can be used and wooden ducks replaced by balls.

Cross Dive Relay

Divide group into teams of equal numbers and have them line up at side of pool. On "Go" one player from each team dives in, swims across pool, gets out on opposite side, dives back into pool, swims back, and *touches off* next player--team finishing first wins. This can be organized as a shuttle relay with half of each team on opposite sides of pool; each player *touches off* his teammate on first trip across pool.

116

Scramble Ball

Divide players into two teams and have them line up on opposite sides of pool; it is advisable for players to be in water with their hands touching side of pool. Instructor stands on diving board, tosses balls or floating corks into water; on command "Go" players try to get as many balls or corks as possible for their teams. Balls or corks collected are credited to the appropriate team, continuing in this manner until one team has obtained the predetermined number.

Potato Relay Race

Divide group into teams of equal numbers and have them line up at ends of pool in shuttle relay formation; floating corks are thrown in water. On "Go" one player from each team dives in pool, secures a cork, returns to his end of pool, and deposits cork in gutter or box; next player from opposite end goes, continuing in this manner until all players on a team have obtained a cork--team finishing first wins.

Additional interest and fun can be derived from this game by numbering the corks. Have an equal number corks with each team's number--the team getting all of its corks first wins. Colors may be substituted for numbers. Different colored corks can be numbered consecutively--each team must collect its corks in numerical order.

Whistle Game

Have players line up along the edge of the pool with their backs to the water; an ordinary plastic or rubber-tip protected whistle on a neck cord (laniard) is thrown into the water. On a given signal players plunge in water and surface dive for the whistle. As soon as a player locates whistle, he comes to the surface and attempts to blow it three times--if successful, he gets a point. Other players try to push the one with the whistle under water so he will drop it. If a player is unsuccessful in locating the whistle, he may hold his hand over his head as he comes to the surface so he will not be ducked. A player is disqualified if he attempts to yank whistle out of another's mouth or gives the no ducking signal when he actually does have the whistle. The first player to obtain a predetermined number of points wins.

Retreiving

Throw a dozen or more objects into the water. Players dive into water and recover as many objects as possible on one trial beneath the surface.

Cage Game

Place cages at two goals about 50 feet apart. Divide any number of players into two teams which line up at their goals and face the center of the pool where a ball has been placed. On signal players swim to ball, and bat, throw, or hit it toward the opponent's cage--a goal counts one point for the team scoring.

Water Baseball

Set up baseball diamond in all deep water, all shallow water, or with only outfielders in deep water. Use indoor baseball and bats, practice golf balls, or ping-pong balls and ping-pong paddles as bats, whiffle balls and bats, or plastic balls and bats--play as regular baseball or softball.

Thread Needle Under Water

Use heavy wooden needle and thread--try to thread the needle under water.

Turtle Race

Use any stroke or skill and swim as slowly as possible through water-- last one to cover designated spot wins.

Shadow Swimming

Have one student swim under water while student on the surface synchronizes his stroke with the one under water. In a clear pool this gives the illusion of a shadow on the bottom--the breast stroke is the easiest to coordinate. Swimmer on top should keep his eye on and coordinate movements with the underwater swimmer.

Horse and Rider

Have one student sit on shoulders of partner. Variations include moving through the water in various ways--forward, backward, sideways, racing, having relays, and doing combative activities. For safety, keep horse and rider near the center of the pool and away from the sides.

Floating Stunts and Exhibitions

The following activities might be considered basic for many aquatic formations and prerequisites for synchronized swimming.

Five Pointed Star

Have five students float with their bodies radiating from a common center. Have them place their feet on an inflated inner tube if necessary. Arms are extended sideward and changed to full extension overhead upon signal.

Short Man Float

Float with only head and feet showing; knees are *drawn* up to stomach and position maintained by sculling. Have student move feet up and down slowly and gradually grow by slowly extending legs to a flat floating position.

Spider Web Float

Have a group of eight swimmers form a circle with four facing in, four facing out, and the tallest students facing the center. Those in the center float, join hands to form the hub, and spread their legs so those on the outer circle can grasp them with extended arms; this forms a wheel which may be turned. If outer circle members float with their legs together, two swimmers may turn the wheel by swimming around and turning it.

Butterfly Floating

Have two students float on their backs next to each other with the feet of one next to the head of the other. Partners grasp each other's nearer leg by placing the nearer hand under the ankle. The pair will turn themselves around by spreading and closing their arms and legs gently.

Double Float

Have partners float on their backs with one in front of the other. Both extend arms over head and keep legs close together; front partner grasps ankles of the other. They slowly and deliberately open and close arms and legs.

Figure Swimming

Execute patterns and figures by using four different strokes; follow the leader as in maze marching or as in any land drill--one in closed or open formation.

The Foursome

Have two students swim on their backs, use crawl kick, and join inside hands with arms stretched sideward. They pull two other students who swim on their stomachs, use crawl kick, keep heads up, and join inside hands with arms stretched sideward.

Burling*

Have two students sit on large, smooth log, and try to unseat each other by rolling the log--*close supervision is necessary for safety.*

Log Walking*

Walk (stand) on log and keep body upright. The student staying on the log the longest time wins--*close supervision is necessary for safety.*

*Recommended for lake use only.

Tug of War

Provide a rope about 30 feet long with loops for 10 swimmers on each team. This is best conducted in the center of the pool and is played exactly like a tug-of-war on land. Be sure to know the ability and skill level of the group before using this activity. Do not permit any student to wrap the rope around his body.

Obstacle Swimming

Much interest, increasing challenge, and a lot of fun can be added to swimming programs for the mentally retarded by introducing a variety of obstacle swimming activities. Activities listed are simply representative examples of the large number which are appealing to and appropriate for retarded students with adequate skill and proficiency in the water.

Swimming in Clothes

Swim while wearing one or more items of clothing.

Swimming in the Rain

Swim one-arm side stroke while carrying an umbrella.

Resistance Swim

Swim and pull boat or canoe which has several people in it. Other objects can be substituted for a boat or canoe.

Towel Race

Swim crawl or back-stroke while holding a corner of a towel in each hand.

Trick Swimming and Sculling

Many of the features of obstacle swimming also apply to trick swimming. In addition, students develop greater confidence in their ability in the water, new and varied coordinations, stronger skills, and prepare themselves for any eventuality which may occur while they are swimming. Care and sound judgment must be used in selecting activities of this type for students with adequate skill and proficiency in the water. Instructors are encouraged to expand this sampling with similar activities with which they are familiar and which are appropriate for their students.

Crab Swimming

Scull backwards from the prone (stomach down) position; flutter kick with toes and hand scull with pushing movements in front of head.

Dolphin Swimming

Scull forward from the prone (stomach down) position with hands at hips, feet together, toes pointed, back arched, and head up.

Torpedo Swimming

Scull from the prone (stomach down) position with feet together and foremost and with toes pointed; hand scull at hips with pulling movements. Use a nose clip at first.

Tasmanian Crawl

Extend arms to side from shoulders, slap water with hands, and scissors kick.

Submarine

Submerge, go to the bottom of the pool, lie on back, extend one foot up, and come back to the surface slowly. The foot with leg extended is pushed up and out of the water like a periscope; swim a short distance with the foot held in this manner, submerge again and repeat. A propelling movement of the arms with palms up will keep the body submerged.

Flutter Scull

Progress forward with flutter kicks aided by hand sculling; may be done on back or stomach.

Reverse Flutter

Use kickboard and kick vigorously with flutter kick; move *backward* instead of forward by hooking the toes.

Marching on the Water

Lie on the back with hands at sides; progress forward with bicycling action of the legs which pulls water slightly towards the body.

Bicycle Swimming

Lie on side with hands placed as if grasping handle bars of bicycle; progress by bicycling movement.

Pendulum

Float on the back with arms extended over head; swing feet slowly downward; when the feet are down (vertical), swing the arms forward and allow the feet to continue backward and upward until floating face down. Reverse the procedure and return to back.

Corkscrew Swimming

Progress forward by executing a half turn on each stroke (keep turning in the same direction). One stroke is made while the body is on the back, the next while the body is on the stomach, continuing in this alternate manner.

Upstream Swimming

Use crawl arm action; go *backward* instead of forward by drawing arms through the water with a minimum of resistance and bending at the hips so the flutter kick drives the body backward.

Crab Breast Stroke

Make breast stroke movements; pull inward very hard with one arm and easily with the other so movement is sideward instead of forward.

Water Walking

Tread water very vigorously with both hands and legs; raise the body as high as possible out of the water and progress forward.

Look Out

Swim a few feet and then lift body high out of the water by vigorously kicking the legs and sculling with one hand; place other hand over the eyes as if looking for someone; repeat several times at various intervals.

Somersaults

Do somersaults (forward, backward, or in combination) continuously.

Walking on Hands

Walk on hands in water about three feet deep. Handstand push ups may be done from this position.

Steamboat

Scull forward with hands below hips; thrash water with a short crawl kick and toot like a tug boat.

Tub

Sit in water with soles of feet together and knees drawn up and out; scull with hands to spin body around.

Water Magician

Take a question from a member of the class; speaker stands directly over the person who is to answer the question and who is lying on the bottom of the pool with his ear against the side of the pool. Speaker stoops and directs his voice to the edge of the pool in order for voice waves to follow the side of the pool; words can be heard if spoken slowly. Student on the bottom then rises to the surface and answers the question.

Novelty Races

In addition to interest, variety, and fun, novelty races provide opportunities for students to practice strokes in many different ways and to develop the ability to react and respond to unusual and unexpected situations in the water. This approach not only promotes confidence but adds another dimension to developing strength, endurance, ability, power, and coordination in aquatic activities.

Ping-Pong Ball and Spoon

Use large wooden spoons and carry ping-pong ball in them according to rules established.

Balloon Race or Ping-Pong Ball

Push balloon or ping-pong ball with face or blow the object. Move the object through the water by splashing and without touching it.

Bobbing Race

Bob width (length) of pool.

Kick Board Race

Use kickboard and progress through water by kicking.

Pennant Relay

Swim on side or back and hold pennant, flag, or similar object in one hand out of the water.

Crocodile Race

Divide group into two teams of equal numbers which line up behind their respective captains. Each player keeps his hands on the hips of the one in front of him; all with the exception of the first player on each team swim with the power of the leg kick. Place the student with the strongest kick last so as to keep the line unbroken. Another variation is to have each player lock his legs around the waist of the one behind him so each can use the arms in either a crawl or breast stroke (last player kicks only).

Chariot Race

Make a chariot from a board or a life buoy. Two students tow another who rides on chariot. The race is a pursuit with one chariot starting at each end of the pool. The object is to continue until one chariot overtakes and passes the other.

Polo Ball Swimming

Swim crawl; push a rubber ball ahead and in front, keeping ball in front of head and between the arms.

Knee Press Race

Swim and hold a rubber ball between the knees. If ball is lost, it must be recovered, placed between the knees and the race continued from that point.

Disrobing Race

Swim with clothes on to some designated point; disrobe as fast as possible and swim back to starting point. A variation requires players to disrobe--dress--disrobe and the next to dress--disrobe--dress, continuing in this manner until all have had a turn. Several sets of clothes are needed for each team.

Novelty Crawl

Swim with aluminum pie shell (plastic plates, paddles, or similar objects) in each hand; swim front or back crawl.

Obstacle Race

Arrange various obstacles in paths of swimmers; prescribe specific maneuvers for each obstacle (go over, under, around, etc.).

Twin Swimming

Have students form teams of two for race with their inner arms locked. A variation is the *Three Legged Race* in which two swimmers have their inner legs locked together. Another variation is to have partners lock legs around each other's hips--both swim on their backs or stomachs.

Ride A Cock-Horse

Have a small swimmer ride on the back of a larger and stronger swimmer; small (top) swimmer sits erect with his legs wrapped around the larger (bottom) swimmer's waist; both swim breast stroke with top swimmer using his arms in rhythm with movements of bottom swimmer.

Stunt and Comic Diving

These activities are primarily for more advanced and proficient swimmers. Many can be incorporated into instructional and recreational programs. Most will add a great deal to demonstrations, water carnivals, open houses, visiting days, and other times when parents and the public visit and view the program. Youngsters like to master these activities and put on shows for other classes and groups within the program. Custodians, cafeteria workers, and other non-pool personnel make enthusiastic and responsive audiences.

Torpedo

Spring from deck or end of pool after running start and plunge into water feet first with arms extended over head. Scull with hands and push body with feet foremost under water; then have feet come up together with toes pointed. Some students should wear a nose clip for this stunt.

Chinese Dive

Stand on diving board with hands together, fingers pointed up, move hands up and down as if praying while squatting and rising (partial knee bends). Spring high into the air, draw legs up as in the frog kick recovery, plunge straight down in water, and come up holding pigtail (hair) in self-rescue attempt.

Applaud Dive

Spring out from diving board, clasp hands in front of body, behind it, and in front before entering water; diver should call out front, back, front as he executes action.

Sitting Bull

Stand on end of diving board in same position as for back dive; bend body forward, keep legs straight, grasp ankles, keep chin to chest, lose balance backward, strike water in sitting position (continue to hold ankles until body touches water).

Ostrich Dive

Spring upward from diving board; place right arm under left leg and grasp nose with left hand, holding this position while in the air--straighten out before entering water. Opposites must be used--right arm under left leg or vice versa.

Immelman Turn

Spring off diving board in a shallow dive; as soon as the body strikes the water turn on back and double back under board. This can be done from the side of the pool rather than the diving board.

Jump For Distance Or Height

Jump from diving board or side of pool striving to go as far out into water as possible. Judge distance by rope or cord to be touched with feet upon entry into water.

The Lookout

Spring high from diving board; quickly place one hand above eyes as in lookout position, place the other hand on hip, hold one foot against the inside of the other leg in crane fashion; drop straight down and enter water feet first.

Cannon Ball

Spring high into air from diving board or side of pool; bring knees to chest and drop into water with a big splash.

Hesitation Dive

Run strongly and confidently along diving board, hesitate timidly and unsurely at end of board, and fall into water.

Sailor Salute Jump

Spring from diving board and on signal (whistle, color, number, shape, letter, word, etc.) salute.

Finale

Indicate the end of a program by having divers wearing single letters dive off the board in order to spell *the end, finis, thank you,* or other appropriate words.

POOL FACILITIES

Children have a ball in a learner pool in New Zealand!

[1]Thanks and appreciation are extended to Merle Dowd, Director of Communications, National Swimming Pool Foundation, 2000 K Street, N. W., Washington, D. C., for his thoughtful review and valuable suggestions and additions to this Chapter.

127

Successful swimming programs for the mentally retarded are conducted
in public and private pools of all sizes and shapes; some are outdoors,
others indoors, and a few are portable. Very few programs are held in facilities designed for instructional swimming or equipped to meet the special
needs of the mentally retarded; the only pools which are available are gra-
ciously accepted and gratefully used. However, as swimming programs for the
retarded become more popular and prevalent, schools, colleges and universities, YMCA's, YWCA's, YMHA's, YWHA's, churches, community associations,
country clubs, and individuals are making their pools available for these
programs. Interested and dedicated personnel from some of these groups are
initiating instructional and recreational swimming programs for the retarded.

Instruction and recreational swimming programs must be adapted to the
facility when existing facilities are used. Generally these facilities can
be made more usable and functional for the program by adding or altering
equipment and reorienting the pool operation to provide the best teaching
and swimming environment for the mentally retarded.

Important to the health and safety of retarded students and to the
success of the program is warm water and correspondingly warm air. Ideally
water should be 80 - 90 degrees and air temperature five degrees above the
water temperature. Water must be clean, chlorinated, filtered, and have an
adequate turnover for the bather-load (see Table 1); adequate checks must
be made to insure proper water chemistry at all times.

Pools should have non-skid floors, decks, and accesses to both shallow
and deep water by ladders or built-in steps; pool bottoms should have very
gradual slopes. Pool depths need to be clearly marked: reaching poles,
crooks, a buoy line separating shallow and deep water, and similar safety
features should be readily available and installed. A large deck area or
substitute dry land space is desirable for drills and other selected teaching approaches.

Adequate shallow to very shallow water areas are important to the success of instructional swimming programs for the mentally retarded, especially
those including the young, timid, and fearful. Some instructors have advo-
cated lowering the water level for some programs to facilitate beginning
instruction. However, in most pools lowering the water level incapacitates
the filter system. The system can be shut down for short periods of time
but it is not considered a wise practice. Lowering the water level one foot
in a large pool represents many thousands of gallons of water and usually
requires a shutdown of several hours to remove the water; refilling usually
takes longer. Most health authorities would frown on lowering the water
level in a pool. A wading pool or some device to raise the level of the
bottom is considered a more satisfactory and effective practice.

Table 1

Proposed Formula for Sizing

Filtration Systems based on Swimmer Density[2]

With the increased use of constant depth training pools and portable pools for physical education and recreation programs, the undefined differences between *light* and *heavy bather loads* have become problematical.

The following formula, based on *swimmer density*--the number of swimmers per 1000 gallons of water per day--is an attempt to define more exactly these differences and to suggest suitable turnover rates.

Swimmers Per 1000 Gallons Per Day	Turnover
7 or less	8 hours
8-15	6 hours
16-35	4 hours
36-50	2 hours
Over 50	1 hour

For example: A 20' x 40' flat bottomed temporary pool with 3' to 3 1/2' of water is used 6 hours per day for an outdoor recreation program. The pool holds approximately 18,000 gallons of water. Fifty swimmers are allowed in the pool during 1/2 hour cycles.

Total bathing load (1 day)	600
Swimmer density (bathers per day per 1000 gallons)	33
Recommended turnover rate (based on chart)	3 to 4 hours

---

[2]This proposed formula is currently being studied by the Committee on Standards and Codes of the National Swimming Pool Institute, 2000 K Street, N. W., Washington, D. C.

Shower rooms, locker rooms, and toilet facilities should be accessible, functional, and usable by the retarded. Every aspect of the facility should be inspected and safety-proofed to eliminate unnecessary hazards. First aid equipment and supplies should be adequate, appropriate, and readily available.

Good public relations make it possible to obtain the use of pools and to make necessary environmental changes--elevating water temperature and satisfying maintenance requirements--which are important to the success of the program.

New Pools

Many organizations are planning multi-purpose community pools which will serve the mentally retarded and those with other handicaps as part of their total program; some pools are being built which will serve the handicapped exclusively. Groups planning swimming facilities should spend considerable time with the pool design in order that a usable and functional facility will be the end result.

The following factors should be considered in planning swimming pools to be used by the handicapped--

General Considerations for the Pool Structure

The pool and pool structure should be easily accessible from parking areas. Walkways, approaches, and halls should be constructed of non-skid materials and should be ramped for changes in elevation. Doors and hallways should be wide enough to accommodate wheelchairs and the passing of heavy equipment. Water fountains, telephones, lockers, and toilet facilities should be accessible from wheelchairs. Locker rooms and shower rooms should be on the same level and immediately adjacent to the pool whenever possible; acoustical tile helps to control noise in indoor facilities. Adequate locker space for all types of handicaps is needed and consideration should be given to providing one or two horizontal locker spaces in addition to conventional vertical lockers. If possible, large padlocks with large keyholes and keys should be obtained for students having visual, neuromuscular or similar problems. Several shower heads and controls should be placed so they can be reached from a wheelchair. Handrails for support should be installed in shower and toilet areas. The extension of toilet-flushing arms permits use by students with various physical handicaps. Shockproof hair-dryers and electrical fixtures are a necessity.

The Pool Area

Many multi-purpose pools have been designed to provide water areas of various depths in order that instructional programs, handicapped swimming, competitive swimming, synchronized swimming, and diving may all be accommodated. There is great freedom in planning an outdoor facility and odd shapes--even free-form--can be set apart in special areas. Indoor pools, however, do not have this degree of freedom in design. Their cross dimension

130

is related to the span of the building. Rectangular swimming areas are most efficient if one is required to relate the total water space available to the span of structure.

Some popular shapes providing multi-purpose areas are L-shaped, T-shaped, H-shaped, and Z-shaped pools. The multi-use pool should be designed so areas may be roped off for special programs. Some pools have been designed so that a movable bulkhead allows the water temperature in the bulkheaded area to be raised independently of the rest of the pool. However, specially designed units such as those described are quite expensive. Often the same purpose can be realized by a separate pool or spa unit with return lines from the heater. This arrangement can give better, more rapid control of water temperature at a lower cost.

There should be adequate deck space all around the pool--deck space should be related to program and to those for whom the pool is designed and used. For example, pools which are used extensively by wheelchair students could have deck space at least the equivalent width of two and one-half wheelchairs. If clear program and participant considerations are lacking, a standard formula of deck/water ratio could be used to determine minimum deck area around the pool.[3] One large deck area should be available, preferably near shallow water.

The area to be used for handicapped swimming should have a depth running from twelve to eighteen inches to four or five feet. Some pool personnel have developed a shallow water area by building a six-foot by eight-foot shelf in twenty-four or thirty-inch water to provide the desired twelve to eighteen-inch depth.

Pools should be designed so as to facilitate getting in and out; flush deck pools have been very satisfactory in this respect. Another design which has drawn favorable reaction provides a water-level deck twenty-two inches wide from the pool edge to the overflow, with the deck area raised six inches above. (See figure.)

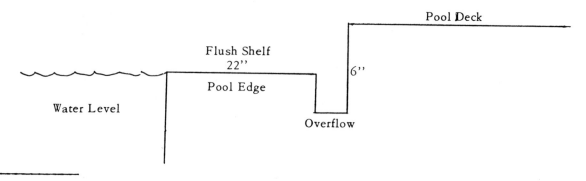

[3]See M. Alexander Gabrielson, Betty Spears, and B. W. Gabrielson, *Aquatics Handbook* (Second Edition), Prentice-Hall, Inc., Englewood Cliffs, New Jersey, 1968, p. 219, for an example of such a formula.

A variety of design treatments of deck level pools is available; likewise there are a number of innovations in recessed gutter type pools. In both of these types, the size, shape, and location of the overflow is of great importance to the operation of the complete recirculating system. In many newer pools, for example, the pictured enlarged *old style* gutter or overflow acts as a surge system which holds water until the pump is ready to send it to the filter. Architects designing such pools are urged to consult with competent hydraulic engineers or swimming pool consultants in the choice of a recirculating system.

Some other modifications which have been used for easy entry and exit are ramps going down into the water or underwater steps with a handrail for support also going down into the water.

The pool should have a good filter-purification system and a heating system capable of raising water temperature quickly. In a multi-use pool some method of bulkheading, as previously mentioned, should be seriously considered in order that the pool temperature in the instructional or therapeutic area can be raised to eighty or ninety degrees to provide a warm pool.[4] Ideally, the air temperature and air flow should also be controlled to prevent evaporation chilling when the student is out of the water. An air conditioning and heating specialist should be consulted on this matter since there is a four to six degree comfort zone--water and air temperature within four to six degrees of each other--which also reduces condensation. A place for hanging towels and robes should be provided in the pool area so students may be dry and warm when out of the pool.

An emergency first aid room with a telephone should open onto the pool deck. This can often be combined with a pool office area.

A storage room opening on the pool deck should be a part of the pool design. This provides a place to store pool equipment and instructional materials which leaves the pool area uncluttered so as to provide a better teaching environment while insuring that teaching aids and equipment are readily available.

Other features that have been found to be valuable include: water inlets opening on the bottom of the pool to provide more uniform temperature throughout the pool; sleeves set in the bottom of the pool for removable rails to be used for support and handholds; a hydraulic or manually operated lift to help non-ambulatory swimmers into and out of the pool; color and sound coding to indicate depths, exits, and other features of the pool; a music or sound system to provide quieting or stimulating music throughout the pool area.

---

[4]Additional information and detailed specifications for this innovation may be obtained from Dr. Frank Papcsy, Department of Physical Education, University of New Mexico, Albuquerque.

Portable Pools[5]

Low cost, pre-fabricated, portable swimming pools are being used in a growing number of American cities to provide needed recreation and swimming instruction to children of inner-city areas. Portable pools are within the realm of possibility and also needed in rural areas where swimming pools—public or otherwise—are virtually non-existent. School physical education programs are being extended and expanded to include swimming instruction through the availability of a wide variety of portable pools. While some camps for the mentally retarded have included portable pools, the potential of this type swimming facility has been relatively untapped in programs for the retarded. Portable pools offer much hope for providing swimming facilities in areas where they are not now available. These pools can be ready on relatively short notice since the time span from inception to use can be expressed in weeks and even days rather than months and years.

The ease with which a specific swimming pool can be carried or conveyed from one place to another is not necessarily a characteristic of all structures described as portable. There are examples where portability is the primary concern and special design and construction problems have been met and overcome to put a swimming pool on a trailer or truck chassis; these instances, however imaginative, are limited. In considering the entire range of portable facilities currently in use, it is more accurate to describe these pools as low cost or pre-fabricated, or intended for temporary, short-term use.

Programs conducted in portable swimming pools are identified more easily by their differences than by their similarities. The pattern of needs, resources and imaginative talents applied to create such programs has varied to such a degree that each program is marked by the character of the community and the individuals who developed it. There is—as yet—no universal blue-print for the use of portable swimming pools. Successful programs, although different in structure and methods, have been marked by urgent needs and imaginative planning by competent physical educators and recreation specialists. Personnel involved in less successful programs using portable pools have lacked the complete planning and trouble-free execution of successful programs. All of these programs—successful and unsuccessful—have been identified by urgency—conventional public facilities were not available and the need for pools was great.

Proper care and supervision in operating and storing portable pools can keep them in serviceable condition for many years. The selection of proper equipment is paramount to the success of a program and care should be taken to choose the specific type and model of pool to meet the specifications of the program. Detailed specifications should indicate size,

---

[5]Information in this section is based upon *Portable Pools*, prepared and distributed by the National Swimming Pool Institute, 2000 K Street, N.W., Washington, D. C.

the degree of portability needed, decking, and other traffic control devices.

The typical portable pool unit consists of metal or wood sidewalls which must be erected on level ground. Water is retained by a heavy gauge vinyl liner which is shaped to fit the supporting sidewalls. The liner is held in position by the sidewalls and the weight of the water. Support walls can be curved (circular, oval, or figure eight) or rectangular. The complete portable pool includes steps, guard rails, filler, chlorinator, cleaning equipment, test kit, and sand; occasionally water heaters are included.

The most common types of portable pools include--

Circular, double-circular (figure eight), oval above-the-ground pools--circular pools have diameters up to 22 to 24 feet and water depth of 36 to 40 inches; oval or figure eight pools are 30 feet long. Units have a high degree of portability. Cost: $1,000 to $1,500.

Modified on-the-ground pools--sizes vary but they are usually no larger than 20 by 40 feet with a depth of 36 to 40 inches. Units have limited portability. Cost: $2,000 to $3,500.

Modified modular in-ground pools--basically an in-ground vinyl liner pool which can be adapted easily and quickly to an on-ground situation. It can be assembled from standard modular panels to almost any size needed. Units have limited portability. Cost: $2,500 to $4,000.

Special institutional pools (vinyl liners)--pool has been designed specifically for public use; 16 by 24 feet by 3 1/2 feet deep. Units have a high degree of portability. Cost: $4,200.

Special institutional pools (aluminum)--pool is all aluminum and does not use a vinyl liner; completely self-contained unit 20 by 40 feet. Units have a high degree of portability. Cost: $22,000.

Whenever portable swimming facilities are used it is important to consider all of the facts in choosing a location. Program needs are important, especially as they relate to traffic patterns and the desires of those to be served. Water, sewage, toilets, security (fencing or shelter), and lighting are equally important operational considerations for placing portable pools. Planning and providing adequate support facilities will help make the facility a successful one and will help in dealings with local health authorities.

The majority of local regulations which govern the construction and operation of permanent swimming facilities are not phrased to accommodate portable pools. In many cases, special rules and regulations have been

drafted to allow the use of temporary pools. This in no way implies that
portable facilities should not be required to meet rigid standards of
operation, but it does indicate that health authorities should be consulted
from the very beginning.

Large scale use of portable facilities should accelerate the acceptance of
this concept. Portable pools used for summer time instructional and recreational purposes should be able to find a winter home in a neighborhood
school, recreation center, or some unused but appropriate community building.

A Learner Pool for Mentally Retarded[6]

Learning to swim has long been emphasized in New Zealand schools. In
1940 the first *learner* pool, a 40 foot by 15 foot concrete structure with a
water depth of 30 inches to 3 feet was built in an elementary school. This
pool was built above ground so instructors would not have to bend too much
to speak to pupils and so timid children would know their instructor was
always close.

Since 1940 nearly 1600 of these pools have been built in New Zealand
elementary schools and have been very successful. Shallow water encourages
confidence; the handrail is never more than a few feet from the beginner;
the water warms quickly and instructors are relieved from the continual
strain of *counting heads*.

At first these pools were of the *fill and draw* type, emptied and refilled
every week; water was chlorinated and tested daily. Ten years ago small
filter plants suited to these pools were developed; most of them are now
filtered and have automatic chlorination. The standard size is now 45 feet
by 18 feet with depths ranging from 30 inches to 3 feet.

Many times during the use of these pools, even 30 inches of water was
found to be frightening to some children. In New Zealand, children begin
school at 5 years of age when some are fairly small. Instructors began
to wonder if even shallower water would be an advantage in the early stages.
In 1965 a learner pool was designed for a school for mentally retarded
children near Auckland.

This pool is similar to the usual shallow pool but has an addition
making it *L-shaped*. The L area is 15 feet long--it could be longer--and
slopes from 9 inches to 30 inches. This depth enables even the most timid
child to lie down in the water, to kick and splash happily--confidence is
very quickly established.

---

[6] This section on *Learner Pools* was contributed by Terry L. O'Connor, 320
Old Illawarra Road, MENAI. N.S.W., 2232, Australia.

The children progress rapidly to hand support with the body and legs floating; with face in the water, they look at the bottom of the pool, pull along with hands on the bottom, and then move to the crawl stroke. Breathing practice is made easier by being able to move forward before actually being able to swim.

Results have been so impressive in this pool that six others of similar design have been built; this is under consideration as a standard pool design in New Zealand. For these situations, programs for the mentally retarded and elementary schools, we are recommending L-shaped pools 45 to 60 feet long by 18 feet wide with a depth of 27 inches to 3 feet for the main pool and an 18 to 20 foot *toe* sloping from 9 to the 27 inches of the main pool. This pool provides for all children from kindergarten age up to 11 or 12 years of age and helps them develop rapidly the confidence so essential to successfully learning to swim.

BEHAVIOR MODIFICATION TECHNIQUES FOR TEACHING SWIMMING TO THE MENTALLY RETARDED

It's fun to be splashed when you have earned it! These youngsters have learned to reserve their "splashes" for those who performed a designated skill. *Happy Day School, Champaign, Illinois.*

Despite the technical and specialized nature of this Chapter, there is important information in it for instructors, aides, parents, and assistants. All can benefit from the second section of this Chapter where practical application of behavior modification techniques for the swimming program is explored in easily understood terms. Instructors should be able to relate practice and theory and to interpret basic concepts to aides and others who work in the program. Consideration should be given to including some of the contents of this Chapter in pre-service and in-service training programs.

Special thanks and appreciation are extended to Constance R. Curry, Director, Happy Day School, Champaign, Illinois; Anthony G. Linford and Claudine Y. Jeanrenaud, Motor Performance Laboratory, Children's Research Center, University of Illinois, Champaign, who collaberated in preparing this Chapter for publication.

Behavior modification is, as the name itself implies, a systematic method of modifying behavior by conditioning operants or acts. These techniques have even been used with considerable success to teach various activities to profoundly retarded. This method can be adapted to teaching swimming and water activities to students classified as low as the bottom end of the trainable scale.

In this Chapter the theory of operant conditioning and behavior modification is reviewed and a theoretical framework is developed and then translated into practical terms--how to use behavior modification to teach swimming.

The Theoretical Framework

An *operant* is simply an act, and an *operant response* an act influenced by its consequences. These consequences may serve to strengthen (positive reinforcement) or weaken (negative reinforcement) the behavior; they may make the behavior more or less frequent. *Reinforcement* itself must be differentiated from reward; in behavior modification it is essential that reinforcement be used. Reinforcement implies *immediate* acknowledgement of the action; reward, on the other hand, is generally used to imply some delayed acknowledgement. For our purposes, delay is fatal--only if reinforcement is immediate will a close association bond be set up between the act and its consequences. As mentioned previously there are two forms of reinforcement--positive and negative. If the consequences of the action tend to increase the frequency of the behavior, it is considered positive reinforcement. On the other hand, if an individual tends to avoid certain consequences, it is considered negative reinforcement. Examples of negative reinforcement are punishment, which should be rarely used because of difficulty in directing an associated avoidance response and because of possible emotional involvement by the student, and removal of an unpleasant situation when a correct response is made. The rat, for instance, soon learns that by jumping a small barrier he can get from the side of the cage that is electrified to one that is not. In effect, he learns to avoid the consequences of staying on the electrified side.

Reinforcers fall into three general categories, *primary, secondary,* and *generalized. Primary reinforcers* are those necessary for subsistence--food, water, avoidance of shock, etc. *Secondary reinforcers* are learned responses caused by pairing a previously neutral stimulus with a primary reinforcer. This is a process similar to *classical or Pavlovian* conditioning. It is essential that the neutral stimulus is presented prior to the primary reinforcer for conditioning to be effective. This kind of conditioning takes place frequently in everyday life--one smells a steak on the barbeque and the smell alone makes the mouth water. Essentially, secondary reinforcement is an *expectancy* procedure. Certain objects or situations can take on generalized reinforcing properties--they can control behavior in a wide variety of situations. Money is perhaps the best example of this, while social praise is another.

In the swimming pool where handing out food reinforcers is not really practical, social reinforcement becomes a valuable tool. However, just patting a child on the head and saying *good boy* can be quite ineffective for the severely retarded child; it simply does not mean anything to him. One does not, however, have to understand fully the language content of a verbal stimulus to respond to it. It becomes possible to apply direct conditioning procedures, to establish the effectiveness of social reinforcers in the very retarded. This can be done during regular physical education classes and in the dressing room. The procedure is always similar--when the child makes a correct response, smile and say *good boy* just prior to giving him the primary food reinforcer. After a while the social reinforcement acquires expectancy of reinforcement properties and becomes reinforcing itself and capable of maintaining or improving behavior in the pool.

The form that the reinforcement takes is also of some considerable interest. There are two basic forms--*continuous reinforcement* where every correct response is reinforced and *intermittent reinforcement* where the frequency of reinforcement in terms of trials and time can be varied according to four schedules:

  a) *Fixed Interval*--reinforcers are dispensed every so many seconds,

  b) *Fixed Ratio*--reinforcers are dispensed every so many trials,

  c) *Variable Ratio* (VR)--reinforcers are dispensed on average every so many correct trials (i.e., on average once every five correct trials--VR5); the subject never knows quite which correct response will be reinforced, this produces a very rapid, increasing rate of responding--the so called *Gambler's Syndrome*,

  d) *Variable Interval* (VI)--reinforcers are dispensed on average once every so many seconds following a correct trial.

VR schedules are response based; VI's are time based. VI schedules produce a consistently high, steady rate of responding. Each of these schedules of reinforcement produces its own particular type of response curve.

Research tells us that in the initial stages of learning continuous reinforcement is best; once a response is fairly well established, a VR schedule is best. Things learned with this schedule (VR) of reinforcement are very resistant to extinction and the schedule itself promotes the highest frequency of response. Under this type of schedule rats have been known to expend more energy trying to gain a good reinforcement than the actual food value that was being provided by the reinforcement.

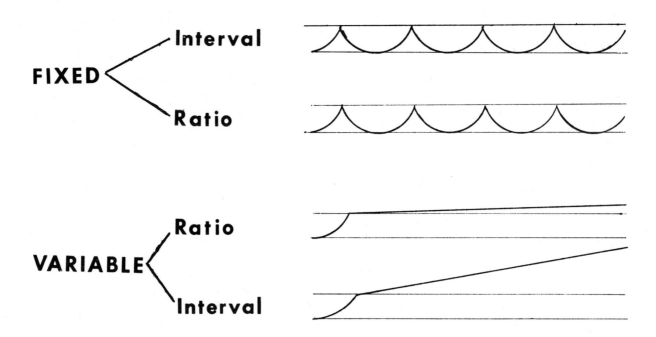

SCHEDULE

RESPONSE INTERVAL

FIXED
- Interval
- Ratio

VARIABLE
- Ratio
- Interval

Thorndike's *Law of Effect* states that those actions which produce pleasant consequences tend to be repeated. In his experiments he only rewarded correct responses. This is in contrast with the more recent work of B. F. Skinner who developed the technique of *successive approximation*--instead of waiting until a final correct response occurred, every response in the direction of the correct response and superior to any previous response is reinforced. This principle is the heart of behavior modification and gave rise to the basic procedure known as *shaping*, the application of the principle of successive approximation in the teaching situation.

For example, we may want to get a child to enter the water. We note carefully his basic behavior which should be stated in the form of a behavioral description and not an inference--"Johnny was angry and afraid when he saw the water" is inadequate for our purposes! We want to know exactly what Johnny did--did he turn away or try to run away from the water? Did he scream, kick, bite? Knowing this, we can task analyze the steps necessary to get Johnny to enter the water starting at his present point. Considerable skill is required in task analysis and proficiency can only be acquired through careful and systematic observation along with a lot of practice. Tasks must be broken down into logical sequences of very small steps or progressions with each step small enough to maximize chances of fairly quick success. These progressions must lead directly to the objective we hope to achieve. Here again the need to be specific must be stressed: an objective such as "to be happy to enter the water" is not good enough. It must be spelled out in behavioral terms--"to grasp the rail and jump off the edge of the pool into two feet of water without exhibiting any inadequate extraneous behavior." This way of stating the objective allows us to see clearly what is required of the individual and to program very specifically for its achievement.

Another frequently employed technique is *fading*. Sometimes it is necessary to give a great deal of adult help to the student to get him to make any response at all. The instructor or aide may have to move the student's limbs manually through desired movements. In swimming, where safety is all important, the fading technique is very useful. Gradually adult help is faded out step-by-step, while the student performs more and more alone. Similarly the instructor's attention can be faded out. Initially the pupil-teacher ratio should be one-to-one. With time, and the use of fading techniques, individuals can be guided into small groups, freeing more staff for individual instruction with other students.

The expectancy properties of secondary and generalized reinforcers were mentioned previously. This can be used in *chaining*, building a chain of behaviors. To establish a chain, always start with the final action of the chain and reinforce its completion. Next, add the next to last action to the final action, continuing in this manner until the chain is complete. Under these conditions, the final action is always reinforced, but more important, each step in the chain brings the child nearer to reinforcement. Because of the *end-to-start* nature of the learning situation, each link leading to the goal acts as a conditioned secondary reinforcer. In other words, the child knows that he is getting closer to the final reinforcer as each link is completed. Further, the completion of each link acts as the stimulus for the performance of the next link. So then, in teaching undressing, first help the child take off all his clothes except the last article; this he does himself after which the action is reinforced. Instructor assistance is faded out at the next article of clothing and the child has to remove the last two, and so on until the chain is complete.

It has been found that responses not reinforced tend to drop out of an individual's behavioral repertoire. Sometimes admonition of undesirable responses provides just the reinforcement in terms of attention, for which the child is looking. One effective way to deal with these situations is to ignore the bad behavior and pay more attention to children who are exhibiting appropriate behavior. However, probably the best way in most circumstances is to try and build up appropriate behavior by conditioning, at the same time bad behavior is eliminated. This usually speeds up the total process considerably.

There are four essential steps to follow if there is to be hope for any success at all--

1. Decide exactly what behavior is expected from an individual.

2. Record his current behavior in specific terms.

3. Analyze the behavior and set up a series of logical steps to progress towards the desired behavior; each step should minimize chances of failure.

4. Re-evaluate the teaching procedures if they result in failure. *Consider failure to be because of the program or task analysis, not because of the participant.*

Practical Application

The first part of this Chapter has dealt with the principles of behavior modification; *reinforcers, shaping, fading, chaining, task analysis, and reinforcement schedules.* This part of the Chapter will look into the practical application of these principles in teaching swimming to the severely mentally retarded. These techniques are applicable to many age groups and not just children. If a child fails to learn to swim by his late teens, frequently this is the fault of the program and approaches, not the individual's ability.

Finding proper reinforcers is essential. When teaching swimming the three main *tangible reinforcers* are the *pool itself, verbal praise and bodily contact* given by the adult instructor and his aides, and the *peers* of those being taught. However, *intangible reinforcers,* success experiences which are very quickly evident in the swimming situation, make teaching swimming to the retarded using the operant approach so rewarding.

Although the three tangible reinforcers are always present in any swimming situation, they must be applied contingent upon the desired behavior as set up by the instructor if they are to be used as reinforcers.

An end goal for an older child who knows how to undress himself but will not because he is used to mother doing it for him would naturally be to have him completely undress himself; the pool could be the ultimate reinforcer for this act sequence. However, there are numerous intermediate goals to be accomplished in which reinforcement must be immediate. Verbal praise and bodily contacts could be used as initial reinforcers for taking off the last article of clothing--such verbal and bodily praise should be contingent upon student success in taking off the appropriate article of clothing. Eventually the individual may be taking off the last four pieces of clothing as a chain is established. At this point two pieces of clothing must be taken off before praise is given for it is not practical to give praise for every little thing done. The goal is to get the student working, with intermittent praise sufficient--continue building in this manner until the student is completely undressing himself. It does not matter how long this takes; the idea is to move as fast as possible with the student always having successes.

Never simply say "you're not going swimming unless you take off your clothes." This approach is far too crude, jumping many steps at once is doomed to failure; such failure must be guarded against. Always start at the precise point you find the student and develop progressions from that point. Behavior modification techniques can be used to teach the student to hang up his clothes--have him hang up only the last article of clothing with the instructor, aides, or assistants hanging up the remainder--continue to praise successes. The next time, have the student hang up the last two articles, and so on, until intermittent praises are producing the desired end result. The importance of moving step-by-step, and being sure the student has completely mastered the previous task before moving to the next one cannot be overemphasized.

Proper use of language is an essential part of behavior modification technique. When teaching the mentally retarded to swim, it is imperative to keep language simple and consistent--the instructor should address the class in short, simple statements, telling the student exactly what is expected of him: "When I say 'go', everybody kick"..."Go!"; "When you hear the whistle, everybody stop"...(whistle blast). "Go" should always be the *one and only* signal to let the student know he is to start and the whistle blast the only termination stimulus. When using praise as a reinforcer, always tell the student exactly what behavior warranted the praise: "Good for kicking your legs"; "Good for looking at me"; "Good for blowing bubbles in the water." An individual may be kicking his legs in the water and shaking his head simultaneously; the latter is undesirable behavior. If simply told "good," the individual may assume it was for shaking his head, thus inadvertently reinforcing undesirable and inappropriate behavior.

Let us assume there is a newly formed swimming class of low trainable retarded students dressed in swim suits ready to enter the water. Some are anxious, others cautious, and some fearful. How can all principles of behavior modification be applied simultaneously? (Assume there is a one-to-one or a one-to-two ratio of instructors and aides to students during the initial stages of the program.)

Start with a simple command such as, "When I say 'Go' everybody hold hands." At this point the behavior of the participant will be shaped, because each instructor or aide will take the hand of one of the students. The student should be praised for holding hands--"Good, David, for holding hands." Next, give a command to go to the side of the pool, using the same approach. (See picture below) Getting the participants into the water may be a little more difficult. The whole procedure must be analyzed and broken down into its component parts, with correspondingly simple commands for each individal step. A sample breakdown of getting students into the water from the side of the pool might be--

1. Give the command to sit--*"When I say go, everybody sit-- 'Go'"*;

2. Give the command to put feet in the water;

3. Give the command to splash yourself;

4. Give the command to splash each other.

Happy Day School, Champaign, Illinois

144

At this point aides go into the pool while the students remain seated at the side of the pool. The program continues--

5. Give the command to hold hands with an aide;

6. Give the command to go into the water.

Start each behavior action with the simple, direct stimulus "Go" and stop the action with a whistle blast; this procedure must be followed rigorously with each command given.

As lessons progress and students begin to respond instantaneously, instructors reduce praise and *fade out* help with the task of getting them into the water. Fade-out is accomplished as the instructor or aide holds only one of the student's hands instead of both of them; then he just touches the hand, and then touches the fingers only. Finally the students get into the water with no help from the instructor or aides at all. This task can be quite easily learned because of the simple, consistent language and the reinforcement provided.

When students are in the water, apply operant principles to teaching swimming skills. Take kicking as an example--it is one thing to know how to kick and quite another to kick with enough force and endurance to hold the body up and to propel it through the water. It is necessary to break kicking down into its component parts as in the following suggested breakdown which progresses from simple to complex[1]--

1. Swing one leg while in a standing position

2. Hold on to the back of a chair or a rail and lift one leg
    and then the other

3. Lift one leg and then the other while in a supine position

4. Lift one leg and then the other while sitting at the edge of
    the pool, lean back on elbows and keep legs in the water

5. Kick while in the water while on the back with an aide
    giving full bodily support (See figure 2)

---

[1]This method has proved effective in a program for severely mentally retarded children at Happy Day School, Champaign, Illinois.

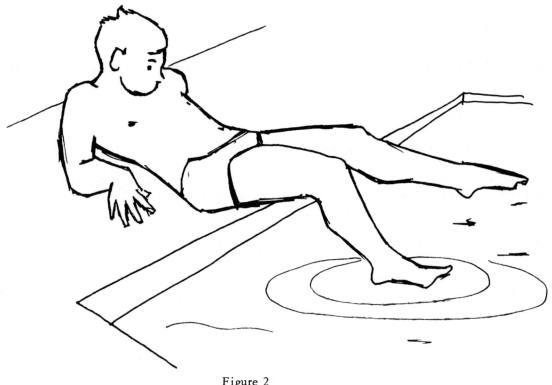

Figure 2

At this point an aide should shape the proper kick by holding the student's legs and moving them through the proper kicking motion. As the student learns to kick, the aide fades out his help in a slow systematic manner. The principle of reinforcement as applied in dressing behavior applies to the kicking situation.

Once the student is kicking independently, build up strength and endurance. This can be accomplished by requiring him initially to kick for exactly five seconds; use a stop watch to insure accuracy. As a reward, give him one minute free time in the pool or allow him to engage in a water game, whichever is more reinforcing for the individual. Gradually increase the length of time of continued kicking using increments of only two seconds if necessary; continue to use the pool as a reinforcer.

One of the most difficult things to teach the low trainable is to float and to recover from this position. Here *fading* of aide assistance can contribute greatly to success. To begin, *shape* the participant into the floating position. (Most low level retardates are afraid of floating; because failure has been conscientiously guarded against, the retardate has developed a necessary trust in the aide working with him, and should be more willing to try to float.) Position your knee to hold up his back; use one hand to direct and hold his head and the other hand to push his legs down or to move his arms into a relaxed position. Once he is relaxed and in the proper position, the fading technique can begin. Start by removing the hand which is used to push his legs down; show the student the hand you have removed and praise him for not needing it. Next, decrease knee pressure for a few seconds at a time. As the student's confidence increases, knee support is used less and less.

Relinquishing hold of the head is the last step, but is by no means a sudden one. It involves a fading out—shaping process of relieving pressure and then touching the student's head, relieving and touching, relieving and touching, until he is floating independently of bodily touch. This procedure may take many, many swimming lessons.

In order to teach recovery once the student is floating independently, back up a step and again hold his head so the chin and mouth are at their highest points from the water. Give the command to the student to bend at the waist--use another person or your free hand and *shape* the bending. Immediately straighten out the individual's legs as he bends; continue to hold the head so his mouth and nose do not go under water. The same principles of fading-out apply in the floating-to-standing recovery. The key point to remember is not to jump from one task to another, but rather to fade-out. While this procedure varies slightly from the normally taught recovery, it has been found in practice to be more effective with the retarded.

Proper hand positions are essential to the mastery of swimming strokes. Many retardates will assume the position shown in figure 3A - position as shown in 3C is desired. The student must be taught to stretch his fingers open and closed (3B and 3C) to get necessary positional feedback. Shape this behavior until the student can reproduce the desired hand position upon command. It has been found ineffective in practice to go directly from position 3A to 3C without the intervening 3B stage.

| Figure 3A | Figure 3B | Figure 3C |

Principles of behavior modification can be applied in teaching the mentally retarded to swim. The key to success in using this approach lies in the ability of the instructor or aide to be consistent in speech, in shaping a behavior, in fading out, and in reinforcing desired behaviors. Build from what the student knows and guard against failure by thoroughly analyzing the skill to be taught.

Games in the water help develop confidence and security. *Happy Day School, Champaign, Illinois*

SELECTED BIBLIOGRAPHY

1. American Association for Health, Physical Education, and Recreation. "The Swimming Teacher's Notebook: A Collection of Ideas, Techniques, and Principles with Practical Examples." *Journal of Health, Physical Education, Recreation,* May 1963.

2. American Association for Health, Physical Education, and Recreation. *Recreation and Physical Activity for the Mentally Retarded.* Washington, D.C.: American Association for Health, Physical Education, and Recreation, and the Council for Exceptional Children, 1966. Chapter 7, "Aquatics," pp. 50-52.

3. American National Red Cross. *Instructor's Manual: Swimming and Diving Courses.* Washington, D.C.: American National Red Cross. (n.d.)

4. American National Red Cross. *Swimming and Water Safety:* Washington, D.C.: American National Red Cross, 1968.

5. American National Red Cross. *Swimming and Diving.* Washington, D.C.: American National Red Cross. (n.d.)

6. American National Red Cross. *Swimming for the Handicapped: Instructor's Manual.* Washington, D.C.: American National Red Cross. (n.d.)

7. American National Red Cross. *Teaching Johnny to Swim: A Manual for Parents.* Washington, D.C.: American National Red Cross, 1963.

8. American Red Cross, Birmingham Area Chapter. "'Sun Dances Inside' After Work with Retarded Children." *Salute,* July, August, September 1966. Birmingham, Alabama.

9. Balch, Roland and Pettine, Alvin. *An Experiment In Underwater Techniques for Non-Swimmers.* Fort Collins, Colorado: Colorado State University, Department of Physical Education, November 1965.

10. Bancroft, Jesse. *Games.* New York, N.Y.: Macmillan Company, 1937.

11. Boy Scouts of America. *Aquatic Program.* New Brunswick, N.J.: Boy Scouts of America, 1965.

12. Boy Scouts of America. *Cub Scout Water Fun.* New Brunswick, N.J.: Boy Scouts of America, 1965.

13. Boy Scouts of America. *Lifesaving.* New Brunswick, N.J.: Boy Scouts of America, 1966.

14. Boy Scouts of America. *Swimming.* New Brunswick, N.J.: Boy Scouts of America, 1963.

15. Brown, Richard L. *Swimming for the Mentally Retarded*. New York, N.Y.: National Association for Retarded Children (420 Lexington Avenue), 1958.

16. Canadian Association for Retarded Children. *Swimming Program for the Trainable Retarded*. (Guide #1--Organization and Administration for the Program. Guide #2--Conducting the Program. Guide #3--Testing and Recognition. Swim Records. Swimming Progress and Achievement Records). Toronto, Canada: Canadian Association for Retarded Children (186 Beverley).

17. Choromanski, Frederick. "Pilot Swim Program Successful in Norwalk." *ICRH Newsletter*, September 1967. Carbondale, Ill.: Southern Illinois University (Information Center--Recreation for the Handicapped).

18. Council for National Cooperation in Aquatics. *New Dimensions in Aquatics, 1966*. Report of the 16th Annual Meeting of the Council for National Co-operation in Aquatics. Washington, D.C.: Council for National Cooperation in Aquatics. pp. 21-23; 91-96.

19. Cureton, Thomas Kirk, Jr. *Standards for Testing Beginning Swimming*. New York, N.Y.: Association Press, 1939.

20. Daniels, Arthur S. and Davies, Evelyn A. *Adapted Physical Education* (2nd ed.). New York, N.Y.: Harper & Row Publishers, 1965. Chapter 15, "Aquatics in the Adapted Program," pp. 439-480.

21. Dauer, Victor P. *Fitness for Elementary School Children Through Physical Education*. Minneapolis, Minn.: Burgess Publishing Co., 1962.

22. Davis, Ernie. "Fresh Approaches for Combating Persistent Problems." *Challenge*, May 1968. Washington, D.C.: American Association for Health, Physical Education, and Recreation.

23. Diem, Liselott. *Who Can?* Downers Grove, Ill.: Gretel & Paul Dunsing, George Williams College, 1962.

24. Diomer, Franklin J.J. "Swim Program." *ICRH Newsletter*, August 1966. Carbondale, Ill.: Southern Illinois University (Information Center--Recreation for the Handicapped).

25. Donnelly, Richard J.; Helms, William G.; and Mitchell, Elmer D. *Active Games and Contests* (2nd ed.). New York, N.Y.: Ronald Press, 1958.

26. Dowd, Merle. Pools in the Schools. Washington, D.C.: The National Swimming Pool Institute (2000 K Street, N.W.). (n.d.)

27. Dowd, Merle. Portable Pools. Washington, D.C.: The National Swimming Pool Institute (2000 K Street, N.W.). (n.d.)

28. Fait, Hollis F. *Special Physical Education: Adapted Corrective, Developmental*. Philadelphia, Penn.: W. B. Saunders Co., 1966. Chapter 21, "Swimming," pp. 262-271.

29. Faulkner, John A. *What Research Tells the Coach About Swimming*. Washington, D.C.: American Association for Health, Physical Education, and Recreation, 1967.

30. Foster, Robert E. "Swimming Activity Opens A New World for Retarded Youths." *Swimming Pool Age*, September 1967.

31. Friermood, Harold, Editor. It's Fun to Swim the Y's Way. New York: Association Press, 1960.

32. Gabrielsen, Milton A., Editor. *Swimming Pools--A Guide to Their Planning, Design and Operation*. Washington, D.C.: Council for National Cooperation in Aquatics, 1969.

33. Gabrielsen, M. Alexander; Spears, Betty; and Gabrielsen, B.W. *Aquatics Handbook* (2nd ed.). Englewood Cliffs, N.J.: Prentice-Hall, 1968.

34. Garrett, Hayward J. "Swimming for the Handicapped." *Illinois News: Health, Physical Education, and Recreation*, May 1966. Jacksonville, Ill.: Illinois Association for Health, Physical Education, and Recreation.

35. Gober, Bill. "Swimming for Trainable Mentally Retarded," *Challenge*, May 1968. Washington, D.C.: American Association for Health, Physical Education, and Recreation.

36. Harbin, E.O. *The Fun Encyclopedia*. Nashville, Tenn.: Abingdon Press, 1960.

37. Hayden, Frank J. "Getting in the Swim," *ICRH Newsletter*, October 1965. Carbondale, Ill.: Southern Illinois University (Information Center--Recreation for the Handicapped).

38. Hindman, Darwin. *Complete Book of Games and Stunts*. Englewood Cliffs, N.J.: Prentice-Hall, 1956.

39. Humbert, Carol and Ryan, Jean. "'Fives' Learn to be Fish with Floatboards." *The YWCA Magazine*, January 1966.

40. Jarvis, Jack. "Seattle Swim Meet is an Annual Event." *ICRH Newsletter*, May 1967. Carbondale, Ill.: Southern Illinois University (Information Center--Recreation for the Handicapped).

41. Johnson, Helene. "Hey! Watch Me!" *Youth Reporter*, October 1966. Birmingham, Alabama: Birmingham Area Chapter, American Red Cross.

42. Kirchner, Glenn. *Physical Education for the Elementary School Child.* Dubuque, Iowa: William C. Brown Publisher, 1966.

43. Lanoue, Fred. *Drownproofing: A New Technique for Water Safety.* Englewood Cliffs, N.J.: Prentice-Hall, 1963.

44. Longview Young Men's Christian Association. *Reports and Proceedings of Annual Workshops in Swimming and Recreation for the Mentally Retarded and Physically Limited, 1962-1969.* Longview, Washington: Longview Young Men's Christian Association (Fifteenth and Douglas).

45. Lowman, Charles L. and Roen, Susan G. *Therapeutic Use of Pools and Tanks.* Philadelphia, Penn.: W. B. Saunders Co., 1952.

46. Murphy, Judy. "The St. Coletta Approach to Swimming." *ICRH Newsletter,* December 1967. Carbondale, Ill.: Southern Illinois University (Information Center--Recreation for the Handicapped).

47. Public Health Service. *Swimming Pools and Natural Bathing Places: An Annotated Bibliography --1957-1966.* (Public Health Service Bulletin No. 1586). Washington, D.C.: U. S. Government Printing Office.

48. Reynolds, Grace. "Swimming and Recreational Programing at the Longview YMCA." *Challenge,* May 1968. Washington, D.C.: American Association for Health, Physical Education, and Recreation.

49. Smith, Hope. *Water Games.* New York, N.Y.: The Ronald Press, 1962.

50. Southern Regional Education Board. *Recreation for the Mentally Retarded: A Handbook for Ward Personnel.* Atlanta, Ga.: Southern Regional Education Board, 1964.

51. Stewart, Joan E. *Participation of Mentally Retarded Children in a Swimming Program.* Master's Thesis, University of Nebraska (Lincoln), January 1966.

52. Vickers, Betty J. *Teaching Synchronized Swimming.* Englewood Cliffs, N.J.: Prentice-Hall. (n.d.)

53. Weiser, Ron, Editor. *Swimming Manual.* Pomona, Cal.: Pacific State Hospital (Rehabilitation Services Department, Box 100). (n.d.)

54. Yates, Fern and Anderson, Theresa. *Synchronized Swimming* (2nd ed.). New York, N.Y.: The Roland Press, 1958.